LOVE MADE ME AN INVENTOR

LOVE MADE ME AN INVENTOR

The Story of Maggy Barankitse:
Humanitarian, Genocide Survivor,
Citizen without Borders

DAVID TOOLE

ORBIS BOOKS

Maryknoll, New York 10545

Founded in 1970, Orbis Books endeavors to publish works that enlighten the mind, nourish the spirit, and challenge the conscience. The publishing arm of the Maryknoll Fathers and Brothers, Orbis seeks to explore the global dimensions of the Christian faith and mission, to invite dialogue with diverse cultures and religious traditions, and to serve the cause of reconciliation and peace. The books published reflect the views of their authors and do not represent the official position of the Maryknoll Society. To learn more about Maryknoll and Orbis Books, please visit our website at www.orbisbooks.com.

Library of Congress Cataloging-in-Publication Data

Names: Toole, David, 1962- author.
Title: Love made me an inventor : the story of Maggy Barankitse :
    humanitarian, genocide survivor, citizen without borders / David Toole.
Description: Maryknoll, New York : Orbis Books, [2025] | Includes
    bibliographical references. | Summary: "Explores the life and work of
    Maggy Barankitse, genocide survivor and founder of Maison Shalom, an
    organization that has cared for orphans and refugees in Burundi and
    Rwanda"—Provided by publisher.
Identifiers: LCCN 2024056638 (print) | LCCN 2024056639 (ebook) | ISBN
    9781626986169 (trade paperback) | ISBN 9798888660713 (epub)
Subjects: LCSH: Barankitse, Marguerite. | Women
    philanthropists—Burundi—Biography. | Catholic
    philanthropists—Burundi—Biography. | Orphans—Services for—Burundi. |
    Orphans—Services for—Rwanda. | Children and war—Burundi. |
    Humanitarianism—Religious aspects—Catholic Church.
Classification: LCC HV28.B37 T55 2025 (print) | LCC HV28.B37 (ebook) |
    DDC 361.7/4092—dc23/eng/20250107
LC record available at https://lccn.loc.gov/2024056638
LC ebook record available at https://lccn.loc.gov/2024056639

For Burundians everywhere,
those who never left,
and those who dream of return

Hope is in the dark, around the edges.

—Rebecca Solnit

Contents

Foreword

It was late 2008, and I was organizing a conference for Christian leaders committed to the work of reconciliation in the Great Lakes region of East Africa. The meeting was to take place in Bujumbura, Burundi, in January 2009. I had gone to visit my bishop in Uganda, Cardinal Wamala, and told him of the conference I was organizing. I asked if he had any recommendations of whom to invite to the meeting. He mentioned a certain woman from Burundi who had recently addressed the cardinals in Rome. He did not remember her name, but he remembered that everyone called her crazy.

That afternoon a Google search for "crazy woman, Burundi" had me reading about Maggy Barankitse and the work of Maison Shalom. I called one of the numbers on Maison Shalom's website and spoke to a young assistant. "No, Maggy is not in the office, but she will call you back." She called later that evening. I was struck immediately by the energy in her voice and by her affectionate humor and easy laughter, and I invited her to the conference.

I was struck again when I met Maggy for the first time at the conference in Bujumbura—by her elegance, by the way she spoke about having "no strategic plan but love," and by how love had made her both a "rebel" and an "inventor." She showed a video of her work in her home village of Ruyigi. I could not believe what I was seeing. Burundi was supposed to be an impoverished country, and the signs of poverty were everywhere. But she was showing images of a cinema, children rollicking in a swimming pool, neat houses, lush gardens, a brand-new hospital. This was totally out of place! I had to go and see it.

That's how it came to be that David Toole and I, along with a few other colleagues, traveled with Maggy to Ruyigi. I am grateful that this initial meeting turned into a lifelong and life-giving friendship between Maggy and David. The book you are holding in your hands is the result of this friendship. Only out of deep friendship can one see clearly and thus appreciate a friend's madness and give an account of it as superbly as David does in this intimate and moving portrait.

As I read *Love Made Me an Inventor*, I experienced the same sense of wonder as the day I first encountered Maggy: how could this be possible? When I traveled with Maggy to Ruyigi in 2009, I listened to her humorous commentary on how crazy we Africans are that we have come to accept the realities of war, ethnicity, and poverty as normal. I saw what she had built in Ruyigi—a swimming pool, a cinema, a hospital—and listened as she explained that the site of the swimming pool had been a mass grave, and that the hospital sat on the ruins of the village where more than sixty members of her family had been murdered in the opening days of the civil war. All the while, Maggy spoke of God's love. It soon became clear that she was no ordinary humanitarian.

Maggy is a theological entrepreneur who has taken all she has learned and experienced about God's love and worked out its social and political implications in a particular context. I've known David Toole for more than twenty years, and I know he is uncomfortable thinking of himself as a theologian, despite his theological training. Not surprisingly, David has not written *Love Made Me an Inventor* as a work of theology. David's portrait of Maggy, however, is inherently theological, because as a gifted writer he has not only paid close attention *to* Maggy's story, but also listened *for* the story behind her life and work.

That story is the story of God's self-sacrificing love: "God so loved the world that he gave his only Son."

For Christians, the cross is a symbol and at the same time the reality of that love. The cross is more than a point of reference for Maggy's life and work. She is, one might say, an "icon" of God's love, which the cross represents. Therefore, I came away from reading *Love Made Me an Inventor* not only inspired by the story of this extraordinary woman but with deeper appreciation for the different dimensions of God's self-sacrificing love for the world. Three of these dimensions stand out.

First, God's love is crazy. In "Trouble," the American poet Jack Gilbert notes that "the pregnant heart is driven to hopes that are the wrong size for this world." That is the trouble with Maggy. She refuses to accept the world on its terms and seeks constantly to interrupt its patterns; she lives as if from another world. For a world that has come to assume the realities of war, violence, ethnicity, and poverty as normal, she cannot but appear to be crazy and dismissed as a "mad woman."

If Maggy has come to accept that label, it is because she says she's learned to be crazy from God. Only a crazy God can send his son to the world knowing he will be rejected and crucified. Maggy understands her vocation as one of inviting others into the madness of God's love. David tells the story of the occasion in 2016 when she invited an audience that included Pope Francis to be crazy like God, reminding them that the first crazy person was Jesus. Pope Francis's response to Maggy was to say, "We need more of this craziness." It is this craziness of love that keeps pressing against the limits of the present with the reminder that the way things are is not the way things have to be. A different world is possible.

Second, God's love is creative. What emerges clearly from David's portrait of Maggy's life is the power of love to invent a different world. What is most remarkable about Maggy's ongoing innovativeness is her excessive attention to detail, beauty, and excellence. Her inventions reflect the scandalous extravagance of God's love; in doing so, they not only confirm that another world is possible, they prove that such a world is not simply a dream. It is real.

Maggy is quick to remind people who admire what she has accomplished that Maison Shalom is not embodied in its buildings or its programs. Maison Shalom is a message: God's love abides, and evil will never have the last word. Love always wins—always creates new life in the space of death, light amid darkness, and goodness in the context of evil. The extravagance, the excess, and the beauty accompanying Maggy's inventions reflect another theological conviction, namely, that for God the only response to an excess of evil is an excess of love.

Third, suffering is integral to God's love. Genocide caused Maggy to experience this dimension of God's love in a personal way in 1993. Her own life was spared, but she was forced to watch the killing of seventy-two people, including her closest friend. Soon after, as she sat crying before the cross in a chapel, she received what she describes as the gift of God's love—the realization that love is our true identity and calling. Maggy's life and vocation are keyed to the gift of God's love, and she has experienced the pain and suffering of the cross that are integral to that gift.

Before her exile from Burundi, when she still lived in Ruyigi, Maggy always insisted on beginning tours of Maison Shalom at the gravesite where she buried seventy-two people. Here, through tears, she would narrate the events of 1993. On my third visit to Ruyigi, I asked her why she insists on going back to the gravesite and to the painful events it represents. She replied that it was not to relive the trauma but to see the future clearly. Christophe Munzihirwa, former Archbishop of Bukavu in Congo, expressed a similar sentiment when he reminded his audience, "There are things that can be seen only with eyes that have cried."

Maggy has cried a lot: through a genocide, a mental and physical breakdown, a life in exile, the destruction of her inventions in Ruyigi, and breast cancer. God's love has not shielded Maggy from pain and suffering. In *Love Made Me an Inventor*, we see Maggy courageously being transformed through the experience of suffering. The key seems to lie in her ability to identify her suffering with God's own tenderness and suffering on the cross. Maggy's own tenderness has deepened through suffering. Her trials and tribulations have not made her angry or bitter but more compassionate and more resolute in her advocacy and struggle with and on behalf of suffering humanity. Greg Boyle, the founder of Homeboy Industries, once noted that "only the soul that ventilates the world with tenderness has any chance of changing the world." Therein lies the mysterious power of love and the strange and painful gift of the cross that Maggy's life illuminates.

God's love has its own logic, which *Love Made Me an Inventor* exposes not in what David has done in telling Maggy's story but in what he was unable to do. David is a clear and systematic thinker and writer who never ceases to seek order and historical precision. Throughout his portrait of Maggy, we see him pressing her for facts, details, and chronology. It is telling, however, that he admits along the way that it is impossible to present Maggy's life in a strictly chronological trajectory. In the epilogue, he describes the challenge: "How do you write about the triumph of good over evil, of hope over despair, when victory looks like defeat?"

David's telling of Maggy's story confirms that the logic of God's love does not follow a sequential, predictable account of time—*chronos*, as the ancient Greeks had it, and thus *chronology*. The logic of God's love is, rather, *kairos*, that is, time not as sequence but as surprise—the surprise of moments when an unexpected gift arrives "just in time." There have been many such unexpected gifts and moments in Maggy's life. Often they have involved suffering and setbacks but never the defeat of love. Instead, for Maggy these moments have revealed new dimensions and opened up unexpected opportunities within the drama of God's love in the world.

The modern notion of "progress" cannot provide a good framework to understand what is going on within this drama. It can be narrated only through the theological register of hope. That is why even though David may not be comfortable describing himself as a theologian, he may have written a work of theology after all, because what he has provided in *Love Made Me an Inventor* is a veritable account of hope (1 Peter 3:15). Without the story and life of someone like Maggy, we would not know what hope looks like.

My hope for readers is that they will come away from reading *Love Made Me an Inventor* not only inspired by Maggy's extraordinary life and work with those at the margins in Burundi and Rwanda but more determined to heed her invitation to become "crazy" like her. In 2016, Maggy received the inaugural Aurora Prize for Awakening Humanity. That Maggy was the first recipient of this award confirms that a radically different future will not emerge without a certain degree of madness, of the sort capable of awakening humanity from the slumber that continues to aid and abet ethnic and racial hatred, greed, and endless cycles of violence.

What Maggy's story confirms is that only a madness grounded in and shaped by the story of self-sacrificing love can offer the world reason to believe that evil will never have the last word. Love always wins. Pope Francis responded to Maggy's story by saying, "We need more of this kind of craziness." After reading David's portrait of "the crazy woman from Ruyigi," I hope you will accept Maggy's invitation to join in her madness.

Emmanuel Katongole

Preface

A few weeks before Christmas 1994, Maggy Barankitse approached the Catholic bishop in Ruyigi, Burundi, and asked for money. Her request was the result of an immediate need: new clothes for her children, a Burundian Christmas tradition. Maggy had no money and two hundred children in need of new clothes—young orphans who had fallen into her care since the outbreak of a civil war now in its second year.

The war had started in October 1993, when a group of Tutsi officers in the Burundian military assassinated the duly elected Hutu president. What followed was an ethnically charged civil war between Hutu and Tutsi that killed as many as three hundred thousand Burundians and created twice that number of orphans. By December 1994, the number of children in the care of "the crazy woman from Ruyigi" was close to seven hundred.

Only the youngest children needed new clothes, but they all needed food; and if the people of Ruyigi had come to see Maggy as crazy in that first year of the war, her constant hunt for food was a contributing factor. When the war started, Maggy was thirty-seven years old and had long been someone who spoke her mind. She once explained this character trait by saying, "We have to let our tongues loose and speak. If I do not criticize, it means I do not love. There is no love without truth."[1]

The opening months of the war altered the terrain of love and truth in Burundi and transformed Maggy. "I became really crazy because every morning I had to find food. Sometimes I lied. I needed milk for the babies, and so I would go to the corner store and take milk and say, 'I will pay you later.' When

I didn't pay and they came for their money, I hid and had the children answer the door. And early in the mornings I went to the fields with children to take corn and other vegetables. We had nothing to eat. I was not afraid to lie. Even to steal."

When the police caught her stealing from fields on public land, she would argue. "You shouldn't try to stop me. You must do this every morning with me. Help me. It's not a crime. It's a lesson that I give you. It's for your children." The police were not persuaded. "They wanted to humiliate me because I am from a prominent family, and they knew me before the war. I was driving a car. I was the secretary of the bishop. I had studied outside the country in Europe. And here I was in this moment, no shoes, no clothes, stealing corn. Sometimes they beat me." Once when the police were beating Maggy, she called out to the children to beat the police, and the children started pelting them with stones. "People came to see. 'Look, Maggy's beating the police.'" Maggy laughs as she tells the story.

Bishop Joseph Nduhirubusa turned down Maggy's request for new clothes for the children. He said the diocese simply didn't have the money. Maggy was undeterred. She knew the bishop had recently put new decorative curtains on his windows, so she slipped into his residence, went into the great hall where he entertained guests, and took down the curtains, leaving in place the lighter, opaque window coverings that hung underneath them. Her seamstress friends then used the material to sew new clothes for the children. When Christmas came, Maggy took the children to Mass dressed in their new clothes. The bishop was presiding. He didn't recognize his curtains.

No one noticed that the children were wearing the bishop's curtains until months later, on March 19. "I remember the day," Maggy says, "because it was the feast of St. Joseph, and the bishop was having a celebration for his patron saint. I was invited and said I would come if I could bring my children." When the children entered the great hall, a nun noticed that their clothes matched the bishop's curtains. "The cut is the same as . . ." she started to say; then she noticed the missing curtains. She made the connection and berated Maggy for what she had done. Maggy replied, "But I did this in December. No one noticed in January or February and now it's March. You didn't see that the curtains disappeared because they are not needed."

That's the same response Maggy offered the bishop when he accused her of stealing his curtains. "No, bishop," Maggy said. "I didn't steal your curtains. I asked you to provide clothes for the children at Christmas, and you did." Referencing the lighter coverings that remained on his windows, she added, "And look, you still have curtains." In the years that followed, as the war raged and hundreds of children turned into thousands and thousands into tens of thousands, Maggy kept finding ways to keep pace with need. When asked how she did it, she would sometimes say, "Love made me an inventor."

~

This book recounts the story of Marguerite "Maggy" Barankitse. In various circles, she is a well-known figure for what she has accomplished through Maison Shalom, an organization she founded in Burundi in 1994, in the opening months of the civil war. For more than two decades during and after the war, Maggy and Maison Shalom focused on caring for Burundi's orphans. Then in 2015, after events in Burundi forced Maggy and the staff of Maison Shalom to flee the country, their work shifted to caring for Burundian, Congolese, and other refugees in Rwanda.

Throughout the world, despite its localized focus, the work of Maggy and Maison Shalom has not gone unnoticed. In 2003, she received the World's Children's Prize for the Rights of the Child, an award Nelson Mandela would win in 2005. In 2008, she was selected as the laureate for the Opus Prize, a prestigious award for faith-based social entrepreneurship. In 2009, France gave Maggy the title *Chevalier* (i.e., knight) in the *Ordre national de la Légion d'honneur*—the country's highest award for both military and civilian service. In 2016, a selection committee co-chaired by Elie Wiesel chose Maggy as the inaugural laureate for the Aurora Prize for Awakening Humanity, "a global humanitarian award recognizing those who risk their own lives, health, or freedom to save the lives, health, or freedom of others." Both the Opus Prize and the Aurora Prize are $1 million awards.

Search Google and you'll find countless stories about Maggy, who turned sixty-eight in July 2024. But aside from short media pieces, a handful of documentaries produced at various points in time, and one outdated biography published in French in 2005, no one has tried to capture the full intricacies of her life and work. *Love Made Me an Inventor* is my attempt to do that, with the caveat that I did not set out to write a comprehensive biography. What I have tried to do instead is create a portrait of Maggy.

When I say I have written a portrait, I have in mind the qualitative research method Sara Lawrence-Lightfoot and Jessica Hoffmann Davis described in the 1990s as *portraiture*. I am not a social scientist, and this book is not a work of social science. Nonetheless, what Lawrence-Lightfoot and Davis said of portraiture is a fitting description of my approach to writing about Maggy:

> Portraits are shaped through dialogue between the portraitist and the subject. The encounter between the two is rich with meaning and resonance. A sure intention in the methodology of portraiture is capturing—from an outsider's purview—an insider's understanding of the scene. The portraitist is interested not only in producing

complex, subtle descriptions in context but also in searching for the central story, developing a convincing and
authentic narrative. The process of creating the narrative
requires a difficult vigilance to empirical description *and*
aesthetic expression.[2]

Vigilance is required, they suggest, because portraiture, by
design, "blurs the boundaries between aesthetics and empiri-
cism in an effort to capture the complexity, dynamics, and sub-
tlety of human experience."[3] In crafting my portrait of Maggy,
I spent considerable time on empirical due diligence, chasing
down the "facts" of her life; but this book is an aesthetic under-
taking anchored in a dialogue I have had with Maggy over the
course of fifteen years.

~

I met Maggy for the first time in January 2009, in Bujumbura,
Burundi, a midsize city that wraps around the northeastern
corner of Lake Tanganyika in central Africa. More than four
hundred miles in length, Tanganyika is the longest freshwater
lake in the world and accounts for two-thirds of Burundi's west-
ern border. The civil war ended officially in 2005 but continued
in fits and starts until the last of the rebels came in from the
bush in December 2008, just a month before I arrived with a
group of colleagues from Duke University.

Our group was hosting a three-day conference on reconciliation and peacemaking in the conflict-ridden region of Africa's
Great Lakes. One of my colleagues had heard of Maggy's work
in Burundi and at the last minute invited her to address the
assembly of seventy or so Christian leaders—mostly Africans
from countries in the region: Burundi, Rwanda, Democratic
Republic of the Congo, Tanzania, Uganda, Kenya, and Sudan.

In a hotel in Bujumbura, Maggy spoke for thirty minutes or
so to conference attendees and then invited those of us staying

in Burundi through the weekend to travel with her to Ruyigi, home to the headquarters of Maison Shalom—a trip of more than three hours on bad roads to the eastern region of the country. Maggy had sketched her story in a hotel conference room, but it was our day in Ruyigi, framed on each end by long drives back and forth across this small war-torn country, that seeded the questions I would spend years pursuing in subsequent conversations with her.

After that first encounter, I met Maggy every year for the next six years in Uganda at what had become an annual conference for Christian leaders in the Great Lakes region. Maggy sometimes came as a keynote speaker and always as an attendee. In between sessions, I pursued my questions. Once during that six-year period, I had the additional opportunity to pester Maggy with questions when she came to Duke University to receive an honorary degree. On that occasion, I shepherded her around campus for a week, listening as she told her story in a wide array of settings—in administrative offices, in classrooms, in television studios, and during formal and informal dinners. In the cracks of her busy schedule, I kept asking questions.

In those years, I didn't know I was writing a book. At first, I was simply trying to make sense of Maggy to stop my own head from spinning. Beyond that I was working toward an essay for another book I was writing about hospitals in Africa. One of the things we saw in Ruyigi in 2009 was the hospital Maggy had recently added to the repertoire of Maison Shalom. A collection of single-story buildings connected by covered walkways, the facility surpassed anything my medical colleagues had seen elsewhere in rural Africa. While giving us a tour, Maggy said a remarkable thing. With great pride, she pointed to the morgue—a prominent presence behind the wards—and proceeded to explain how this building was positioned in relationship to the others, suggesting, it seemed, that the morgue had been key to the design of the whole hospital complex.

Earlier, Maggy had taken us to the hospital's pediatric wing, which included a neonatal unit with state-of-the-art incubators. When showing us the morgue, Maggy said, "It was more expensive than pediatrics. All the people told me I was crazy, but for me it is not a hospital. It is a sacred place." Many of my conversations with Maggy for the first six years flowed from the bewilderment I experienced in that moment, because I couldn't find a way to make sense of a hospital designed around a morgue. In time, my sense-making became the outline of an essay that turned into a presentation I gave in classrooms and faculty meetings, at academic conferences, and for public audiences.

Then in May and June 2015, a dramatic event shifted the course of Maggy's life, forcing her to leave Burundi. Maggy and I had met in Uganda in January that year, and I had recorded a long interview, a finale of sorts, with wrap-up questions for my essay about the hospital she had established in Ruyigi. What happened in May and June, however, ensured that my interview was not a finale.

In July 2016, I traveled to Kigali, Rwanda, to hear firsthand about what had led Maggy—and most of the staff of Maison Shalom—to flee Burundi a year earlier. I spent several days with Maggy and the staff, witnessing the axis of their work shift from children in Burundi to the tens of thousands of Burundian refugees who had flowed over the border into Rwanda during the previous year. What all this meant for Maggy, who had escaped from Burundi with only a handbag, wasn't clear. What was easy to see, however, was that her previous successes were not sufficient to protect her from the full force of becoming a refugee and joining the world's sixty-five million displaced people.

I'm not sure what I would have done with Maggy's story after my visit to Rwanda if, a little over a year later, Maggy had not called me unexpectedly and announced that she was in Atlanta at the Carter Center with extra time in her schedule. She had noticed that Durham, North Carolina, was only a one-hour flight away and suggested that she fill the time by coming to visit me. She arrived soon after, and for three days my wife, Nancy, and I welcomed her into our home. Nancy took her shopping and made sure Maggy made it to daily Mass at the local Catholic church. For my part, I invited her to accompany me to the classes I was teaching and arranged meetings for her on campus.

During that visit, I began to see that something profound had happened. Maggy was a refugee living in exile, trying to make sense of her life, with a growing awareness that her circumstances were pressing her into something new. That had been true even before she fled Burundi, when friends had called upon her to speak out not only for children but for her country against a repressive government. But what I witnessed during her impromptu visit was the start of an even more significant transition.

Throughout our time together—in classrooms, at the dinner table, and sitting on my living room couch—I witnessed Maggy working out in real time how circumstances had changed her life. She had fled Burundi in June 2015 and received the Aurora Prize in April 2016. It was now September 2017. She was beginning to settle into the realities of exile and had marked the receipt of the Aurora Prize as a crystallizing moment for her vocation. The combination of exile and the award left her troubling through what it would mean to dedicate herself not solely to caring for children, nor to speaking out for a country, but to the work of awakening humanity.

Even after more than eight years of conversations with Maggy, I still didn't know I was writing a book, but I certainly sensed more to the story I had been telling about Maggy, and I started trying to work it out. I was still working it out in April

2022 when Maggy returned to Duke to present an invited lecture. Her visit had been scheduled for 2020, but the pandemic caused a two-year delay. Had she come as planned, I may never have written this book.

In a way I can't quite articulate, the pandemic had a profound effect on how I viewed Maggy's story and was the impetus for me to turn what had been an essay on a hospital into a book about Maggy. Maybe it was because the pandemic put the future in question and Maggy's life had long been a testament to how to live in the face of an uncertain future, or maybe it was simply an awareness that none of us have unlimited time on this planet. Certainly, I had been assuming that another opportunity for conversation with Maggy would always arrive. After the pandemic, however, I saw her upcoming visit as an occasion for asking final questions and finding some definitive way to end my telling of her story.

Maggy stayed for a week. I interviewed her in public for the keynote event and at my dining room table, and I carried on conversations with her whenever her schedule allowed, including a memorable session in the lobby of her hotel, during which she acted out her daring escape from Burundi. Here again, as in 2015, was the finale. When she departed, I started writing, taking advantage of the freshness of her voice and the transcripts from a final interview in which I had asked her my lingering questions. Soon I had finished a draft of a small book, but that is not the book you hold in your hands, for two reasons.

First, Maggy's life took another dramatic turn when she was diagnosed with cancer just days after she left Duke in April 2022. Second, I couldn't find a publisher for the manuscript I had finished. While Maggy was in treatment for breast cancer, the story I had written about her life was languishing, at first in the hands of an agent and then in a proverbial drawer. By the time I renewed my efforts to find a publisher, two years had passed, and Maggy's story had moved on again, which led me back to Rwanda in July 2024.

This time, Nancy came with me, and we spent ten days with Maggy and a collection of remarkable Burundians, refugees all—including some from the diaspora for whom Maggy has become a gathering force. Because I now had a publisher with a production schedule and a deadline, the conversations I had with Maggy were in fact the finale I thought I had orchestrated twice before, in 2015 and 2022. The trip proved essential not only because it allowed me to catch up with what had transpired in Maggy's life and work since 2022 but, even more, because I was reminded that Maggy the humanitarian and citizen without borders is inseparable from Maggy the Burundian genocide survivor who now lives in exile in Rwanda—where reminders of genocide are everywhere.

It's something like standard protocol when in Rwanda to visit a few of the more than two hundred genocide memorials spread around this small country—a testament to the fact that during the hundred days of killing in 1994 people truly had nowhere to hide. I had traveled to some of the memorials on previous trips to Rwanda, but visiting the memorials while staying with Maggy, a genocide survivor from a neighboring country, was a reminder that Maggy's universal message of hope and humanity is inextricably bound to the turbulent history of Burundi and Rwanda. All the world may be a stage, as Shakespeare had it; but for the many parts Maggy has played upon that stage, all the exits and entrances belong to Burundi and Rwanda.

~

In the end, Maggy's story is one without borders, but it never escapes the gravitational pull of its origins in two of the smallest countries in Africa, each the size of a postage stamp relative to the vast geography of the continent. Sitting just south of the equator—Rwanda atop Burundi—both countries are dwarfed by their immediate neighbor to the west, the Democratic Republic of the Congo, which spreads out across the center of the continent for more than nine hundred thousand square miles.

Compressed between the expanse of Congo to the west and Tanzania to the east, Rwanda and Burundi each occupy barely ten thousand square miles of Africa's landlocked interior. Imagine Alaska sidled up next to Vermont and Massachusetts and you have some sense of scale, except Congo is 36 percent larger than Alaska, and the population density of these two small African countries is more than twenty times that of Vermont.

Although Maggy now spends most of her time in Rwanda, her story begins in Burundi, where a population of nearly fourteen million tries to eke out subsistence in a country that competes for being the poorest in the world. One visitor to Burundi in 2010 offered an apt description: "If my months here are any indication, [most Burundians] are probably poor; most likely illiterate; guarded toward their neighbors; skeptical of their leaders; not at all unkind; worried for their children; unsure when the next meal will find them; hopeful, impossibly hopeful; and generally glad to be tilling their soil and drinking their banana beer and making do in whatever thrifty, belt-tightened way, if only there could be a few good leaders and a small dose of good luck to help this country back on the right track."[4]

That was when things were looking up after a devastating civil war. The years since have brought neither luck nor leaders. Burundi is known as the land of milk and honey, which is descriptively apt—cows and beehives are prevalent; but as a biblical allusion it is now entirely aspirational. Nonetheless, Maggy's hope remains that her country will once again be a land of promise and paradise. She knew it as such when she was young in the early years of independence.

From her grandfather and others of his generation, Maggy had also heard of earlier times when all was well with the world, before the Germans and Belgians showed up. The Germans arrived in the 1890s, the Belgians in 1916, as Germany was on its way to defeat in World War I. The Belgians stayed until 1962. It's not incidental that Maggy was just five years old when Burundi won its independence from Belgium, nor that her grandfather was born in 1898, when Burundi was a precolonial kingdom just coming into the grip of the German Empire.

When pressed about the origins of her tendency to let her tongue loose, Maggy says that it began as early as she can remember, when she was a young girl of five or six. Even then her family would say to her, "You make too much noise." The memory turns into a story about her grandfather and the times she would argue with him about milk, which he held especially dear because of his traditional Burundian commitment to his cows.

When Maggy found that she had been given too much milk to drink, she would say, "It's too much. I can't finish."

"Then give it back," her grandfather would reply.

"No," Maggy would say. "I will give it to the people who have only cassava to eat."

Her grandfather would protest, "It's milk for my cows, not for people."

Sometimes Maggy's retort would be, "How is it that you know the names of all your cows but not the names of your grandchildren? If you want somebody to obey you, call your cows." Sometimes she would invoke the Lord's Prayer. "I prayed this morning 'Our Father. . . .' We must provide as we've been provided for." Then off she would go to give away her extra milk to people in need.

Maggy stops to explain that her grandfather was not Christian. "Of course, he accepted baptism, but he was not really

Christian. He attributed all Burundi's problems to 'those evil missionaries' and to the Belgians. He hated the Belgians so much." It's often in stories Maggy tells about her grandfather that the complexity of her own life shows up. She was born into the tangled world of a precolonial past and a colonial present, and she came of age in its postcolonial unraveling. The first parts of that story are an essential prologue to hers because just past these pages you will encounter descriptions of horrific acts of violence. Knowing how things came to be that way might both soften the shock and open the heart to paradise lost.

Prologue

Richard Burton and John Hanning Speke arrived at Lake Tanganyika on February 13, 1858. Their journey from the east coast of the African continent had taken more than seven months and covered nearly a thousand miles. Arab traders trafficking in slaves and ivory had established the route as early as the 1830s. As word of the lake had spread, so had the possibility that it might be the source of the Nile River, the wellspring of Egypt's storied civilization. Long a matter of European curiosity, the search for the origins of the Nile had become an obsession by the mid-nineteenth century.[1]

Burton saw the lake for the first time from the summit of a nearby hill: "The whole scene suddenly burst upon my view, filling me with admiration, wonder and delight. Nothing, in sooth, could be more picturesque than this first view of the Tanganyika Lake, as it lay in the lap of the mountains, basking in the gorgeous tropical sunshine." Almost as striking was the human activity that saturated the scene: "Villages, cultivated lands, and frequent canoes of the fishermen on the waters give something of variety, of movement, of life to the landscape."[2]

After settling into Ujiji, a way station for slaves and ivory passing from the interior to the coast, Burton headed north on the lake, traveling up the eastern shore with a small number of men in two large canoes. On the fifth day, they arrived at "the southern limit of Urundi." There, Burton met a "minor chief," whom he learned was subject to "the mwami or sultan of Urundi."[3]

Burton also learned that this was as far as he could go. "The inhospitality of the Warundi and their northern neighbors allows neither traffic nor transit to the north. Here, therefore, the crews prepare to cross Tanganyika."[4] As he prepared for his own crossing, Burton was unaware that he had just touched the edges of a remote kingdom, a complex society centuries in the making that had organized itself against the Arab slave trade and the encroachment of outsiders.

The *mwami* Burton had heard of was Mwezi Gisabo. He had been king for almost a decade and would remain so until the Germans deposed him in 1903. His kingdom advanced from the lake into the rugged hills and mountains to the north and east. On its northern border was another kingdom, similarly organized, the one Burton had heard of simply as the Warundi's "northern neighbors."

No non-African, non-Arab outsider touched upon the kingdom of Burundi again until the American explorer Henry Morton Stanley arrived in 1871, after finding the long-lost David Livingstone in Ujiji. Still searching for the source of the Nile, Stanley and Livingstone followed Burton's course up the eastern shore of the lake. Unlike Burton, they made it all the way to the north end, where, Stanley reported, "The natives had yet never seen a white man."[5]

Like Burton, Stanley was completely taken by the landscape: "Our canoeing of this day was made close in-shore, with a range of hills, beautifully wooded and clothed with green grass, sloping abruptly, almost precipitously, into the depths of the fresh-water sea, towering immediately above us, and as we rounded the several capes or points, roused high expectations of some new wonder, or some exquisite picture being revealed as the deep folds disclosed themselves to us. Nor were we disappointed."[6]

As with Burton, people were part of Stanley's wonder: "Every terrace, small plateau, and bit of level ground is occupied. The steep slopes of the hills, cultivated by the housewives, contribute plenty of grain, such as dourra and Indian corn, besides cassava, ground-nuts or peanuts, and sweet potatoes. The palm trees afford oil, and the plantains an abundance of delicious fruit. Nature has supplied them bountifully with all that a man's heart or stomach can desire."[7]

Stanley and Livingstone stayed in the area for ten days and traveled a bit farther north on the Ruzizi River to confirm that it was an inlet and not an outlet to the lake, discounting the lake as the source of the Nile. They were well received by the leaders of the settlements on the north end of the lake, who passed on considerable detail about the physical and political geography of the region, naming numerous leaders and the areas of their purview.

"All these countries," Stanley reported, "are only part and parcel of Urundi, extending over ten days' journey direct north from the head of the lake, and one month in a north-eastern direction. Direct north of Urundi is Ruanda; also a very large country."[8]

~

No white men showed up in the region again until 1892.[9] Stories, however, had been let loose. When Burton and Speke left Lake Tanganyika in 1858, Speke had not given up searching for the source of the Nile and spent the next five years traveling north into what's now Uganda and South Sudan. Writing of his travels in 1863, he offered an origin story for the people of the region, whom he divided into two types: rulers who herded cattle and subjects who worked the fields. The former, he said, had originally lived farther north in Ethiopia (also known then as Abyssinia) and had migrated south.

"I propose to state my theory of the ethnology of that part of Africa inhabited by the people collectively styled Wahuma," Speke wrote. "It appears impossible to believe, judging from the physical appearance of the Wahuma, that they can be of any other race than the semi-Shem-Hamitic of Ethiopia."[10] Here Speke was drawing on a long European tradition that Ethiopians were descendants of the biblical figure Ham, one of Noah's sons.[11]

Speke adapted this tradition to conclude that the cattle-herding Wahuma had come to the region from Ethiopia as outsiders: "In these countries, the government is in the hands of foreigners, who had invaded and taken possession of them, leaving the agricultural aborigines to till the ground, whilst the junior members of the usurping clans herded cattle." Speke added that the Wahuma could also be found much farther south, in the hills "overlooking the Tanganyika Lake," where "their name became changed from Wahuma to Watusi."[12]

～

The German explorer Oskar Baumann traveled to the king-doms of Burundi and Rwanda in 1892. It had been more than thirty years since Speke passed near in 1858, and more than twenty since Stanley and Livingstone touched on the west-ern edge of Burundi in 1871. Traveling west from the coast, Baumann crossed into "completely unknown territory" in late August. "We were able to make inquiries for the next few days' journey," he reported, "but beyond that lay Urundi, a country with which there was no communication at all and about which only dark rumors reached abroad."[13]

Over the next five weeks, Baumann became the first white man to step foot in Rwanda and to traverse a sizable portion of Burundi's interior. Writing of "high grassy mountains cov-ered with the dark dots of settlements," Baumann described Rwanda as "that fabulous land that many travelers had heard of but in which no one had ever set foot." Following Speke, he wrote also of "Watussi with completely Abyssinian faces. Every-where there were Watussi, who immediately stood out because of their slim build and almost European type."[14]

When Baumann arrived at the north end of Lake Tangan-yika after three weeks of travel, his description was reminiscent of Burton's first sighting of the lake: "The view is one of the most magnificent I have seen in Africa. Before us stretched a huge inland sea, the deep blue Tanganyika with its thundering, ocean-like surf. Behind the lush, palm-fringed shore, the green Urundi mountains rose in the east."[15]

Baumann spent only a few days in Rwanda. But in 1894, the German explorer Gustav Adolf von Götzen spent five weeks traversing the full breadth of the kingdom, which he described in ways reminiscent of Burton's and Stanley's first encounters with Burundi:

> The dark slopes, as well as the bottom of ravines and saddles, are usually covered with lush banana groves or fields of sorghum, beans and peas, between which countless round huts can be seen. Next to the huts, which often have a fence at the front, there are also pumpkin and tobacco beds. The population density is extraordinarily high. Farmsteads line up one after the other, and there is hardly a piece of land between them that has not been used for some kind of cultivation or as pasture. The livestock is very well looked after. Well-stocked bean fields with large shoots that took the place of bean poles, then again sorghum plantations in which scarecrows—replicas of men shooting arrows—had been set up. All this had aroused our wonder.[16]

Götzen's observations about the social order in Rwanda were similar to Baumann's. "We find a large mass of the agricultural rural population who have been settled there since ancient times, the Wahutu. Everywhere it was easy to distinguish this indigenous Negro population from the ruling Wahuma." Götzen noted, however, that despite clear distinctions, "masters and subjugated are almost completely assimilated in customs and traditions." He also observed that everyone spoke the same language: "There is little to be found of the Hamitic element, an original language of the Wahuma: the immigrating conquerors have—as in so many similar cases—subordinated themselves linguistically to the natives."[17]

~

Between 1896 and 1899, the Germans followed up these two exploratory expeditions with seven progressively robust military incursions. In August 1896, Capt. Hans von Ramsay established a military post in Burundi on the north end of Lake Tanganyika. It was a modest affair, staffed with only eleven soldiers. Then in September, Lt. Col. Lothar von Trotha spent a month marching troops across Burundi, which he deemed "the paradise of the colony."[18]

Ramsay returned to the region in 1897, for a three-month incursion intended to force both Burundi and Rwanda into the colonial fold. He succeeded in Rwanda, where the king agreed to place his kingdom "under German protection," but he failed in Burundi.[19] Mwezi Gisabo, who by 1897 had been in power for almost fifty years, continued to resist outsiders, just as he had when Burton showed up on the edges of his kingdom forty years earlier.

The German response to Mwezi Gisabo's recalcitrance was to unleash more military force against the Warundi. Heinrich von Bethe led an expedition in 1898. Bethe recorded the results. In one instance, "Thirty-six Warundi were killed, 10 were made prisoner and, judging from the bloodshed, many people must have been wounded." A few days later, "The losses incurred by the enemy amount to 84 dead, a large number of wounded, and 36 prisoners, to which should be added 16 head of cattle and 400 head of small livestock." The following day, Bethe reported, he had "all the houses burnt."[20] All that in the year Maggy's grandfather was born.

Bethe returned in 1899. This time he destroyed six of Mwezi Gisabo's residences, with the result that "the king fled."[21] In the ensuing months, Lt. Werner von Grawert, an adjunct to Bethe, continued this campaign, during which he earned the nickname Digidigi, an attempt to capture the sound of the Maxim machine-gun that was part of Germany's colonial toolbox. Grawert's troops burned everything they could, announcing as they did so, "It will be like this every day until the chief admits defeat."[22] It took four more years, but in 1903 Mwezi Gisabo conceded to the Germans.

The Germans still had work to do to get their way in Burundi, but in the space of a decade they had set an inescapable course for the future, one defined by a series of navigational errors. The historian Jean-Pierre Chrétien offers a helpful summary. When figures like Speke, Baumann, and Götzen arrived in the region, Chrétien says, they "saw, above all, aristocracies in power," but they "missed the cultural dimension, that of beliefs and rites involved in kingship. What escaped them, in other words, was how this institution ultimately took root in the popular imagination. The colonizer was more interested in division and moralizing than in trying to understand. Little by little, the ancient logics lost their meaning, and by the end of the period the monarchies had vanished: what remained were empty shells."[23]

That's a summary of a long story, but it gets to the punch line, which is that, in the span of a few decades, first the Germans and then the Belgians replaced a complex precolonial social order with the simplicity of an ethnic divide. Overlaying Speke's conjecture on the observations of Baumann, Götzen, Ramsay, and others, Germany and Belgium assumed that the Tutsi were a superior race that had migrated from the north with their cattle, subjugated indigenous Hutu farmers, and raised up kings and kingdoms. When colonial efforts weakened and deposed the kings and dismantled the complex social order of their kingdoms, all that remained was the myth of ethnicity. Exactly how that played is not a prologue to Maggy's story but an integral part of it.

PART ONE

(East of) Eden

And the Lord God planted a garden in Eden, in the east; and there he put the man whom he had formed. Out of the ground the Lord God made to grow every tree that is pleasant to the sight and good for food, the tree of life also in the midst of the garden, and the tree of the knowledge of good and evil.

—Genesis 2:8–9

Cain said to his brother Abel, "Let us go out to the field." And when they were in the field, Cain rose up against his brother Abel and killed him. And the Lord said, "What have you done?"

—Genesis 4:8–9.

A child may ask, "What is the world's story about?" And a grown man or woman may wonder, "What way will the world go? How does it end and, while we're at it, what's the story about?" I believe that there is one story in the world, and only one, that has frightened and inspired us. Humans are caught in a net of good and evil. There is no other story.

—John Steinbeck, *East of Eden*

On October 25, 1993, Maggy Barankitse buried seventy-two bodies in a mass grave. She knows the number because, she says, "I counted." The site was a makeshift cemetery near the compound of the Catholic bishop in Ruyigi, Burundi. A day earlier, Maggy—stripped naked, beaten, and tied to a chair—had watched as the people she was now burying were murdered in a fit of ethnic violence. For the burial, Maggy had the help of a few men from the local prison and Chloé, her oldest daughter. They moved the bodies from the bishop's compound to the grave site in a wheelbarrow and worked in a hurry, fearful that the perpetrators would return.

Among the dead was Maggy's friend Juliette. She was wrapped in the altar cloth from the bishop's chapel. Maggy had retrieved the cloth reflexively, a spontaneous attempt to rejoin Juliette's head with her body. The day before, a machete blow had separated one from the other, just after Juliette had asked Maggy to care for her one- and three-year-old daughters, Lydia and Lysette.

Before they departed, the killers had freed Maggy from the ropes that bound her to the chair. After they were gone, she gathered up Lydia and Lysette and thirty other surviving children and left the compound in search of safety and shelter. As she was leaving the scene, the same reflex that would later prompt her to turn an altar cloth into a burial shroud caused her to grab Juliette's head from the ground. "It was hard to go with Juliette's head, but I couldn't bear to leave my friend behind."

I first heard the outlines of that story on January 17, 2009, when a group of colleagues and I went with Maggy to the site of the mass grave. We arrived at the small, unkempt cemetery on the outskirts of Ruyigi about 2:15 in the afternoon. The gray of the morning had given way to a blue sky half full of shape-shifting clouds. The cemetery glowed green in sunlight, with knee-high grass and weeds entangling weathered wooden crosses. Much later I would learn that some of those crosses marked the graves of mothers and infants who had died of AIDS while in Maggy's care.

The focus of the moment, however, was the mass grave. Capped by a concrete slab decorated with white tiles, it sat toward the middle of the cemetery. We followed Maggy as she picked her way across the cross-cluttered space to a drab stucco memorial that rose from the concrete like a giant tombstone. We stopped there, as Maggy stepped up onto the grave's overlay and began to tell us what had happened in the compound of the Catholic bishop on October 24, 1993.

On the face of the memorial just behind Maggy as she spoke, we could see the words of the famous Prayer of St. Francis, in French:

> Seigneur, faites de moi un instrument de votre paix!
> Là où il y a de la haine, que je mette l'amour.
> Là où il y a l'offense, que je mette le pardon.
> Là où il y a la discorde, que je mette l'union.
> Là où il y a l'erreur, que je mette la vérité.
> Là où il y a le doute, que je mette la foi.
> Là où il y a le désespoir, que je mette l'espérance.
> Là où il y a les ténèbres, que je mette votre lumière.
> Là où il y a la tristesse, que je mette la joie.
> Ô maître, que je ne cherche pas tant
> à être consolé qu'à consoler,
> à être compris qu'à comprendre,
> à être aimé qu'à aimer.

I recognized enough French from graduate school to be able to pick out *make, peace, love, truth,* and *joy,* and guessed at cognates like *instrument, discord, pardon,* and *console.* The rest came clear when I looked up the prayer in English:

Lord, make me an instrument of your peace!
Where there is hatred, may I bring love.
Where there is offense, may I bring forgiveness.
Where there is discord, may I bring harmony.
Where there is error, may I bring truth.
Where there is doubt, may I bring faith.
Where there is despair, may I bring hope.
Where there are shadows, may I bring light.
Where there is sadness, may I bring joy.
Oh Master, grant that I may seek rather
    to console than to be consoled,
    to understand than to be understood,
    to love than to be loved.[1]

Over time, I have come to understand that this is Maggy's prayer, and that in Maggy the Lord has answered it. I write this as someone who is not convinced that there is a Lord who answers prayers. Nonetheless, Maggy Barankitse is convincing.

According to the date stamps on my photographs, it took Maggy seven minutes to tell the story of the events that led her to bury seventy-two people in the mass grave around which we were now gathered. When she got to the part about Juliette, she held up side-by-side pictures of Lydia and Lysette as small children and as young women, letting us know, without quite saying it, that she had fulfilled her promise to her friend. She did not tell us on that occasion about taking Juliette's head with her as she led the children to safety, or about hiding it from Lysette that night, or about taking the cloth from the altar in the chapel the next day to use as a burial shroud, or about what she said to God in that moment, or about having to identify Juliette's body and that of her husband by their hands and the rings on their fingers, which she removed and gave to Lydia and Lysette when they were older.

These intimate details came later, during the many conversations I would have with Maggy in the years to come, as her story became something of an obsession of mine—not because of what she said while standing on the mass grave but because of something she said a few hours earlier.

~

Before Maggy took us to the cemetery, she gave us a tour of the sites around Ruyigi that, in the years since 1993, had become the physical embodiment of Maison Shalom—the House of Peace—the organization she had founded to care for Burundi's orphans.[2] The tour included a visit to Rema Hospital, which had opened just a year earlier. As we drove there, Maggy stopped the cars in our procession and had us get out so that she could show us the hospital from a distance.

The high ground in front of us, Maggy said, was Nyamutobo Hill. We could see the hospital sprawled across the flat hilltop. Maggy pointed to a building standing apart, a hundred yards to the left of the hospital. A small maternity center. She had built that first, she said. Then she explained that the hospital sat on the site of her family's village, which was destroyed in the opening salvo of ethnic violence in 1993, two days before the massacre she had survived in the compound of the Catholic bishop.

We had stopped in the middle of the road so that Maggy could give us perspective. She wanted us to know that during the war the site of the maternity center had been the preferred location of the army's artillery battery and that the hospital sat on the ruins of her ancestral village.

Maggy often says things that are hard to process in the moment, when her words first hit your ears. I remember distinctly that as we walked from the cars to the entrance of the hospital one of my colleagues asked her if we had heard correctly. Had she really built the hospital on the ruins of the village where most of her extended family had died in October 1993? "Yes," she responded, adding, "I will show you where my mother's house used to be."

That was just a few minutes before we encountered the hospital's morgue and, as I described in the preface, had tried to process not only that Maggy had built her hospital on the ruins of her village but also that she had designed the whole complex around the morgue. This encounter with Maggy and Rema Hospital was a disorienting experience, so much so that in the months that followed I experienced something like intellectual vertigo. It was in that state that I began chasing down the details of Maggy's story.

~

The town of Ruyigi sits in the eastern reaches of Burundi, sixty miles west of Bujumbura and the shores of Lake Tanganyika. Tanzania is less than twenty miles to the east and south, and the Rwandan border is seventy-five miles due north. Most people have heard of the Rwandan genocide, even if the details have faded over the decades. But what transpired in Burundi is largely unknown, perhaps because, viewed from the outside, it was less dramatic: not a hundred-day rampage that left as many as a million people dead and millions more displaced, but a drawn-out war that, alongside the HIV/AIDS epidemic, produced hundreds of thousands of dead and a greater number of orphans—all in a country roughly the size of Maryland with a population of six million in 1993.[3]

Of course, for people who lived and died in Burundi between 1993 and 2008, the Burundian experience was all too close to that of Rwanda, with the added burden that it went on for years with no end in sight. Maggy's story is inseparable from what transpired in Burundi in October 1993 and from the long war that followed, but that's not where it starts. Maggy marks 1972 as the beginning of her story.

"People think I started in 1993, but, no, I started in 1972, when I was sixteen. I was away in secondary school in Bujumbura when Tutsi began to kill Hutu. They killed some of our teachers, and some of my classmates lost their fathers, but the school didn't tell us to pray, even when we were in church. They had no compassion. I remember I couldn't sleep, and I cried all night. I decided to leave school and return home."

At home, Maggy confronted her mother, Thérèse: "Tell me why they killed our teachers. You say we are all children of God. How, then, in a Catholic school are they not able to protect the teachers?" Growing up, Maggy explains, she heard little of Hutu or Tutsi. "My mother took me to church every morning before school. She taught me humility and compassion and that we are all one family, so I didn't understand why people were killing one another." The ethnic violence of 1972 so stunned Maggy that she refused to return to school, saying to her mother simply, "You lied to me."

René Lemarchand has called what happened in Burundi in 1972 "a forgotten genocide."[4] A report the following year summarized the harsh realities. "Through the spring and summer of 1972, in the obscure Central African state of Burundi, there took place the systematic killing of as many as a quarter million people. Though exact numbers can never be known, most eyewitnesses agree that over a four-month period, men, women and children were savagely murdered at the rate of more than a thousand a day."[5]

The proximate cause of this genocide, in which a Tutsi-dominated military killed thousands upon thousands of Hutu, with a focus on educated men, was a Hutu-led uprising. Lemarchand describes the bare-bone details: "On April 29, like a bolt out of the blue, anti-Tutsi violence swept across the lakeside town of Rumonge. In a matter of hours, the rebellion spread to other localities along the shore of Lake Tanganyika, including the southernmost town of Nyanza-Lac, where roving bands of Hutu attacked Tutsi civilians. In the provincial capital of Bururi, all military and civilian authorities were killed. After taking control of the armories in Rumonge and Nyanza-Lac, the insurgents proceeded to kill every Tutsi in sight."[6] The insurgents numbered about a thousand. Over a few days, they killed roughly the same number of Tutsi—and Hutu, too, when the latter refused to join in the killing.

The violent response of the Tutsi-led government was immediate, but it took a few weeks of administrative organization for the killing of Hutu to become genocide—and to show up for sixteen-year-old Maggy in the disappearance of her Hutu teachers and in the silence of her Hutu classmates who had lost their fathers without avenues for understanding or spaces for their expression of grief.

Faced with Maggy's accusation that she had lied, Maggy's mother responded the way any parent of a teenager would: "And where will you go? If you want to change this society, you must study." Then her mother said something else: "If you've suffered so much, wait. Wait." The meaning is unclear until Maggy finishes the story. "You see, we were in the village, with no electricity. But in Africa, you have seen, we have these small bottles, and we put in oil and a wick and light them with a match. In Burundi we call them *colloboi*. Sometimes, when my mom wanted to read the Bible, or to pray, she would use these for light. She brought me one and said, 'When you are abandoned, you can be this.' What I often repeat comes from my mom. 'Be a light in the darkness.'"

Having heard Maggy utter these words many times, I say, "So this is the image that you carry, the one that defines your life." Maggy replies, "This is it," adding, "but you must not be too bright. You don't want to become a rebel. Just a small light wherever you are." It's unclear if that was part of her mother's message or something Maggy had to learn about light—and about waiting in darkness.

When darkness enveloped Ruyigi and Maggy in October 1993, Maggy's mother was not there to support her. She had died of cancer in 1989. Maggy is clear, however, that her mother was the most significant influence on her life: "I was lucky to have an extraordinary mother. She never went to school. She was a farmer. But she always found ways to answer my questions, and she laughed at me when I thought I was more clever than she was."

Given where Maggy's life was tending already when she was five or six and arguing with her grandfather about giving milk away to people in need, it's perhaps not insignificant that Maggy's mother was an orphan. "Her father died when she was a baby," Maggy says. "Then her mother returned with the baby to her family. When she arrived, she also died, leaving my mother an orphan to be raised by my grandmother." Maggy sums up the story with a biblical reference. "My mom was the Benjamin of her family."

When Maggy's father died, her mother was only twenty-four. It would have been customary for her to remarry, but she didn't. Instead, she raised her two children—Maggy and a younger brother—as a widow. And yet, Maggy says, children were everywhere. "We were so many in the house, and I never heard my mom say she had only two children, because of my cousins." Maggy and her brother sometimes got jealous. One day they complained. "You give the best things to our cousins." Maggy's mother responded, "What's important to you, the things I give you, or my love? I didn't remarry because of you. I stay here because of you. And now you accuse me of not giving anything to you, but I give you love, which is the best thing."

Summarizing the impact her mother had on her life, Maggy says, "It's like a legacy. My grandmother took in my mother as an orphan, because when there is death in the family, that's what you do. And then my mother took in my cousins. When I started taking in orphans, it wasn't a sacrifice. It was normal, a family heritage."

~

Although a Hutu-led uprising had been the spark for the 1972 genocide that caused Maggy to call her mother a liar, the resulting conflagration had been building almost since the day Maggy was born. She simply didn't know it. In part, that was because her mother had inoculated her against the myth of ethnicity with daily trips to morning Mass and messages about a single human family, and in part it was because when she was born in 1956 that myth had not yet taken hold in Burundi as it had in neighboring Rwanda.

Maggy's first memory of a world divided between Hutu and Tutsi is one of confusion. It was 1961. She was five and in her first year of school. One day a representative from UNHCR (the United Nations Refugee Agency) came to her classroom and called for all Rwandans to follow. "I followed," Maggy says, and then explains. "Before colonization, our problems were not ethnic. There was a king and a kingdom made up of clans. All the clans had a role to play in the kingdom. We didn't care about Hutu and Tutsi. Conflicts were not ethnic but between clans. My clan is Banyarwanda, which is also how we refer to Rwandans in Kirundi. I followed because I was thinking, 'I am Banyarwanda,' but they stopped me and said, 'No, Banyarwanda from Rwanda, not from Burundi."

The teacher must have explained that the Rwandan children were refugees, but when telling the story, Maggy skips that step. "I was confused. When I got home, I went to my grandfather and asked, 'Why are there refugees? Why can't people live in their own country?' And I remember my grandfather accused the Belgians. He hated the Belgians."

The Rwandans in Maggy's kindergarten class were the children of Tutsi refugees who had fled Rwanda during the Hutu revolution, which took place between November 1959 and July 1961. I wrote in the prologue, following Jean-Pierre Chrétien, that the monarchies in Rwanda and Burundi had vanished in the course of German and Belgian colonialism. Although a helpful punch line, the reality was more complicated. In fact, the Belgians ruled Ruanda–Urundi indirectly as a single colony through both monarchies, with Rwanda as the prototype.

Aidan Russell explains: "Belgian authorities viewed Rwanda with admiration as the model of a sophisticated African monarchy, structured through what they regarded as a rigid ethnic hierarchy. The neighboring kingdoms, therefore, were degraded and corrupted versions of this mistaken image."[7] The image was a mistake because, following the myth that had taken root in the colonial mind, the Belgians misread the Rwandan social order as anchored in ethnicity. What the image got right, however, or at least approximated, was that in Rwanda power was centralized in a Tutsi monarchy. The Belgians doubled down on that reality, warping it with the myth of ethnicity, with the result that Hutu, by far the majority, were relegated to the social, political, and economic margins. Then in 1959, after decades of Belgian rule through the Tutsi monarchy, the Hutu orchestrated a revolution.

Led by the Parti du Mouvement de l'Emancipation Hutu (PARMEHUTU), the revolution toppled the Tutsi monarchy. The last king—Kigeli V—fled the country in January 1961. Rwanda gained its official independence from Belgian rule eighteen months later in July 1962. Unfortunately, the PARMEHUTU rhetoric during the revolution set the tone of what was to come from a Hutu-dominated government. PARMEHUTU's stated goal was "to restore the country to its owners," and if that made the Tutsi unhappy, then they should "return to Abyssinia."[8] What tens of thousands of Tutsi did instead was flee across the border into Burundi, where the Belgians continued to rule through a Tutsi-dominated government. It was this mass exodus of Tutsi from Rwanda into Burundi that led to Maggy's encounter with the refugee children in her kindergarten class.

Like Rwanda, Burundi gained its independence from Belgium in 1962, but the monarchy continued. Then in April 1965, when Maggy was eight, Hutu officers in the army launched a coup against King Mwambutsa IV and the Tutsi-dominated government. The coup failed, its leaders were executed, and widespread repression of Hutu communities followed. Fifteen months later, a second coup succeeded, led not by Hutu but by a Tutsi officer named Michel Micombero. He deposed the king, abolished the monarchy, and became president of the First Republic. Maggy had just turned ten.

I asked Maggy about her memories of this time, when she was eight and nine and ten and Tutsi–Hutu tensions were growing. I was trying to figure out why 1972 came as such a shock to her, given the tumultuous events and significant violence in 1965 and 1966. "Did you simply not hear of these things," I asked, "from your parents or on the radio?"

"Well," Maggy replied, "in 1965 was the first time I saw things. I could see in school for example a suspicion between teachers. In my village we were only Tutsi. The Hutu were in another village. I could see a difference; but when I was small, I was thinking that at some point we'd all be together. When I asked my mother what was happening, she didn't talk about Hutu and Tutsi but about some people not believing in the love of God. My mother protected me. But in 1972, that was a horrible thing, to see Hutu killed, and Tutsi . . . " Maggy left the next words unsaid, adding only, "I suffered."

～

René Lemarchand has called Rwanda and Burundi "genocidal twins," an apt description of the way in which the 1959

Hutu revolution in Rwanda led to genocidal violence in Burundi in 1965 and 1972, which in turn influenced the 1994 genocide in Rwanda.[9] If twins, however, these two neighboring kingdoms-become-countries are fraternal not identical, which is something the Belgians missed. By privileging the Rwandan model of monarchy, into which they imported Speke's Hamitic narrative about the superiority of the cattle-herding pastoralists, the Belgians erased the complex texture of Burundi's pre-colonial social order, which was not a replica of Rwanda's, in part because the ruling aristocracy was neither Tutsi nor Hutu but Ganwa, a royal lineage that produced kings.

Again, Aidan Russell explains: "In neighboring Rwanda during the nineteenth century the royal dynasty identified as Tutsi; almost all the powerful were Tutsi, even if not all Tutsi were powerful. But in Burundi, the Ganwa aristocracy was more ambiguous. Some legends made them Tutsi offshoots, others suggested their dynastic founder had been Hutu. In practice, their social distinction set them apart from both."[10] Notably, Burundi also had a judicial institution that worked against any simple divide between Hutu and Tutsi. Within every community there were people known to be wise and just who acted as adjudicators of justice. They were called *Bashingantahe* (ba-*shingan*-high) and could be either Tutsi or Hutu; moreover, they stood outside the monarchy and had the authority to call the king to account.[11]

If Burundi lagged behind Rwanda in letting *Tutsi* and *Hutu* loose as ethnic categories that could hold life and death in the balance, it was because parts of its precolonial social order persisted, and for Maggy they showed up in her grandfather, whose impact was a close second to that of her mother. Born in 1898, Jean-Paul Mushungu became a great chieftain during Belgium's tenure in the region, and he put his people on guard against the Belgians. Because coffee production was a Belgian idea, he used to pour cow urine on coffee plants to kill them. Now when Maggy drinks a cup of coffee, she sometimes thinks of her grandfather.

Maggy's father, Michel Barankitse, was a postal worker for the Belgians and died of an unknown illness when she was five, before she started school. When she did start school, her grandfather enrolled her, and he made two changes to Maggy's biography. He moved her birthday from May 21 to May 20, because the latter date is the day Belgium celebrates its birth as a nation. He also changed her name from *Habyonyimana* to *Barankitse*. In a country where traditional naming practices do not include surnames, Habyonyimana was Maggy's given name. She explains the change to Barankitse: "My father's death was very hard on my grandfather because he loved my father so much. I remember when my father died, my grandfather looked to my fifteen uncles and said, 'Why do you stay and it's Michel who died?'"

Maggy had fifteen uncles because her grandfather had six wives. When the missionaries came, he chose one and dismissed the other five. One of the five not chosen was Maggy's paternal grandmother. She departed for Uganda, leaving her son—Maggy's father—behind. "I think my grandfather changed my name to Barankitse because in his mind he was preparing me to replace my father." Both of Maggy's names would turn out to be fitting: Habyonyimana means *It is God who helps me*, and Barankitse can be translated variously as *They blame you; they are against you; they are boxing you in*.

"I am the daughter of my mother and my grandfather," Maggy says. "I can be kind, and I can be a rebel. I think I have succeeded because I have put the two together." She explains by telling a story about a time her mother gave food to a poor woman for her children. Later, Maggy saw the woman selling the food in the market and ran to tell her mother: "Mama, you gave food to Emily to feed her children. But she lied to you. I found her in the market. She's selling all the food you gave her. You are so naive. They always lie to you. You give them food and clothes, but they sell them." Maggy's mother laughed and responded, "Maggy, if you've never been lied to, you've never been kind. Don't come again to tell me I am naive."[12] Maggy makes sure I understand the story. "Because of my mother, I am kind, but I am not naive. When people lie to me, I think of my grandfather. When I don't want to be like my grandfather, I think of my mom."

~

In abbreviated public summaries of her life, Maggy doesn't say quite so much about her mother and grandfather. She says even less about her education and how it was linked to the events that transpired in Burundi between 1972 and 1993. When Maggy refused to return to school in 1972, her mother had said, "You must go and become well educated." Maggy's grandfather's reaction to her refusal to return to school was to discipline her for even thinking she had a choice.

Maggy's response to her grandfather, in perfect keeping with who he had formed her to be, was to rebel. "No, I will not return." Instead, she moved from the boarding school more than three hours away in Bujumbura to a school in Rusengo, only ten miles from Ruyigi. "I wanted to be near my mom." She had also decided to become a teacher, because it seemed like the best way to rebel against what she had witnessed in her school when her Hutu classmates lost their fathers and her Hutu teachers disappeared and no one said anything. "I couldn't accept that."

Maggy spent the next seven years at the École normale Rusengo, first completing her secondary education and then studying to be a teacher. When she graduated in 1979, she took a teaching job in Ruyigi. Over the next decade, she left Burundi twice to study in Europe. First, she went to Lourdes, France, for three years of theological education, and then to Fribourg, Switzerland, for two years of training in business management. Both stints in Europe were the result of roadblocks she encountered in her chosen profession.

In 1981, Maggy was fired from her teaching job in Ruyigi because, with her twelve- to sixteen-year-old Hutu and Tutsi students, she produced and directed a play critical of the government. The president at the time, Jean-Baptiste Bagaza, was a Tutsi. He had conducted a successful coup in 1976, ending Michel Micombero's decade in power. Harboring the same fears of a Hutu rebellion that had led Micombero to unleash the genocide in 1972, Bagaza spent the next decade trying to shore up the minority rule of Tutsi. Maggy's innovative teaching was an affront to that effort. "I was expelled for being insolent," Maggy says, "for sowing seeds of civil disobedience, for preparing a rebellion."

Never one to be inconsistent, Maggy had displayed her insolence two years earlier when, at the age of twenty-three, she adopted her first child. Chloé was one of her students and was crying in class. Maggy learned that Chloé's mother had just died and that she had lost her father to the genocide in 1972. Chloé was a Protestant Hutu from the south. Maggy was a Catholic Tutsi from the north. "I refused to accept that because a student was born on the wrong hillside, they had no future."

Maggy's response to her sudden unemployment in 1981 was to approach Joachim Ruhuna, one of Burundi's two archbishops who previously had served as the Catholic bishop of Ruyigi. "I think I would like to help you," Maggy said to him. Ruhuna replied, "Help me? But you are so young; you don't understand."

Maggy countered, "No, I understand. I want to create a new generation in Burundi. We Burundian Christians, *we* don't understand, that's why we have been lying for such a long time, and we don't denounce what's going on." Fifteen years later,

Ruhuna would be assassinated for denouncing violence and refusing to take sides between Hutu and Tutsi in the civil war, so perhaps it's not surprising that his response to this twenty-four-year-old schoolteacher who had just been fired for civil disobedience was to say, "I will send you to Lourdes for theological education, and then you can teach religion in our schools."

When Maggy returned from her training in France in 1984, she took a job teaching religion in the SOS Children's Village in Gitega, the historic capital of Burundi an hour's drive west of Ruyigi. SOS Children's Villages were the creation of Hermann Gmeiner, an Austrian who devoted himself to caring for the nearly sixteen million homeless children wandering around Europe after World War II.[13] Writing in 1960, Gmeiner said of Europe's orphans, "They had no chance of a normal upbringing in the ruined cities and large refugee camps. Many people were seriously worried about the problem of the lost children. No one thought of the simple, natural solution—to give these children a normal life again. Not life in an orphanage or any other kind of institution, but life in an ordinary house with a hearth, a living room, and a bedroom, where the child could live with a resident 'mother' and with other children who would become his 'brothers' and 'sisters.'"[14]

Gmeiner built his first houses for orphans in Austria in 1949. In the following decades, he spread the model around the world. Burundi would eventually harbor five of Gmeiner's villages.[15] Founded in 1976, the village in Gitega was first. When Maggy started working there in 1984 her charge was to put her theological education to work teaching religion to sixteen- to eighteen-year-olds in a vocational school.

Gmeiner was a committed Catholic, but schools affiliated with SOS Children's Villages were not Catholic schools; rather, they were designed to teach orphans the religion of their biological family or, if no biological family remained, then the religion of the wider culture. In the 1980s, Catholicism was far and away the dominant religion of Burundi, with almost 70 percent of the population identifying as Catholic and no other religious tradition capturing more than 8 percent of the population.[16] This reality made the school at the SOS Children's Village in Gitega effectively a Catholic school populated by a mix of Tutsi and Hutu orphans—seemingly the perfect setting for Maggy to enact the aspiration she had conveyed to Bishop Ruhuna: "I want to create a new generation in Burundi." It didn't take long, however, before Maggy ran into problems, one of which was Gmeiner's model. It was completely out of step with Burundian culture.

Years later, when Maison Shalom was absorbing thousands of Burundi's orphans and circumstances were forcing Maggy to be creative, she developed a model that stood in direct opposition to what she had experienced when teaching in the SOS Children's Village at Gitega. But that's to get ahead of the story. The more immediate problem Maggy faced between 1984 and 1987 was the ongoing presidency of Jean-Baptiste Bagaza, who was fearful that, left unchecked, the Catholic Church might educate a generation of Hutu who would grow up to take over the country from the Tutsi minority. Many priests were Tutsi, but 85 percent of Burundians were Hutu, and the church was ever present in communities throughout the country, not least as an educational institution.

Almost as soon as he came to power in 1976, Bagaza worked to marginalize the Catholic Church, not because of any theological disagreement (he was Catholic), but because he saw the church as a threat to his political power. In 1977, he banned the broadcast of all religious programs; in 1978, he denied diplomatic passports to Catholic bishops; in 1979, he made it illegal to hold prayer meetings in homes and started deporting missionaries. In 1985, he declared success and doubled down. "We have reduced the influence of the Catholic Church, and we shall reduce it further."[17]

The next year, Bagaza went after church-affiliated schools. First, he moved all secondary schools under state control; then he abolished Catholic catechetical schools, which functioned as the preferred primary schools for many Hutu. By 1987, it was illegal to teach religion in schools, which is what Maggy had been doing in Gitega in the three years since returning from Lourdes. Once again, Maggy lost her job and changed course. "I decided to help my village. That's when I went to Switzerland."

Maggy spent the next two years in Fribourg studying business administration. With her village in mind, her focus was on "sustainable development," a field just surfacing at the time, as part of the global agenda.[18] "I wanted to show that it was possible to transform, to develop my village, so when I returned from Switzerland, I began to bring water and electricity." Maggy also started working half time for Joseph Nduhirubusa, who had replaced Joachim Ruhuna as the bishop of Ruyigi when he became archbishop of Gitega in 1980.

"I told the bishop I wanted to work for him," Maggy explains, "and he hired me to work in the diocesan office of development." Once she had settled into the job, Maggy's routine revolved around her life in the village and her work for the bishop, which expanded to include being the diocesan secretary. The Cathédrale des Martyrs de l'Uganda and the bishop's residence were on the far side of town from Maggy's village. Maggy often made the walk of about a mile in the company of her adopted children, by then numbering seven—four Hutu and three Tutsi. For four years, Maggy made this walk, splitting her time between the village and the diocese—until October 24, 1993: "The day my life changed completely."

～

Two days earlier, on the morning of Friday, October 22, Maggy woke up in her village on Nyamutobo Hill and walked with her seven adopted children into Ruyigi. Maggy was headed to her job at the church, and the children were on their way to school, except Chloé. Now twenty-six and attending university, she was home on holiday. When they arrived in town, they found that school had been canceled, and then Maggy heard the news: a day earlier, a faction in the Tutsi-led military had assassinated the Hutu president Melchior Ndadaye. The first democratically elected president of the country, he was just three months into a five-year term.[19] With warnings from people in Ruyigi that vengeful Hutu were wreaking havoc on Tutsi villages in other parts of the country, Maggy went to the bishop's residence to retrieve valuable documents related to her adopted children. Then she headed back to her village, telling Chloé to gather food and take the children to the bishop's residence.

When Maggy got to the ravine that marks the low point before the gentle rise of Nyamutobo Hill—near the place she had stopped to show us the maternity center and the hospital—she could see that her house and other houses in her village were in flames. Convinced she could stop whatever was transpiring, she continued toward the village, but she met members of her family and others fleeing, and they were adamant that it was too dangerous for her to continue.

Maggy was stranded on the road, unsure of what to do, when Chloé arrived with her six siblings. They had come searching for Maggy. With increasing chaos and her village on fire, Maggy tried to join others in flight. She asked family members if she could join them. They replied, "Not unless you leave behind your Hutu children." Hutu, after all, were at that moment destroying their village. Maggy refused.

Moving on, she encountered some Hutu who were headed for the nearby Tanzanian border. She asked if she could join them. "Only if you leave your Tutsi children here." Maggy's village had become an inferno. Ruyigi had disintegrated into a free-for-all. And no one wanted anything to do with Maggy and her Hutu and Tutsi children. "Suddenly we were alone."

Maggy decided to go to the bishop's compound. Along the way, she met her good friend Juliette Bigirimana, a Tutsi married to a Hutu. Juliette was a nurse; her husband, Cyprian Ndimurwanko, was a physician. They had two young children. "Come with me to the bishop's compound," Maggy told Juliette. "I am a Tutsi with both Tutsi and Hutu children. You are a Tutsi married to a Hutu. We must be prophets. Now is the time for us to show people that Tutsi and Hutu don't need to kill each other."

By evening Maggy, Juliette, Cyprian, and all the children were in the bishop's compound, along with a growing number of others, mostly Hutu. What followed were thirty-six hours of anxious limbo. "Many people came to bring news from the hillsides," Maggy says. During this time, she and some of the priests made forays into town. "We tried to help the best we could, still hoping the catastrophe was limited to what had already unraveled throughout the hillsides."

~

By Sunday, October 24, well over a hundred people—a mix Hutu and Tutsi—had found refuge in the bishop's compound. The bishop was out of town. In his absence, the vicar general was there, as a standard step-in when the bishop traveled. About 9:00 a.m., Maggy and others were preparing breakfast and planning for Mass. Rather than risk the quarter-mile walk to the cathedral amid the continued chaos and confusion in town, they had decided to stay and celebrate Mass in the garden outside the bishop's residence.

Looking out a window from the great hall of the residence, Maggy was the first to see what appeared to be a mob of Tutsi climbing the fence into the bishop's compound. She told everyone to run or to hide, suspecting that it was more than a mob. The Burundian military had long been led by Tutsi; and the day before, Maggy had watched a military plane land in Ruyigi. "Normally the military protects all the people, but the arrival of the military in Ruyigi meant that revenge was going to be hard." That was the lesson of the 1972 genocide, when the Tutsi-dominated military organized killing squads with specific instructions to target Hutu, especially Hutu intellectuals. "That's why I told the father of Lydia and Lysette to go hide in the ceiling." Cyprian did not need convincing. His father had been a victim of the pogrom against the Hutu in 1972.

The vicar general, like Maggy, a Tutsi, crawled under a bed. Maggy tried to hide, too, in a way that later became laughable: she and eight other women tried to fit under a single bed. When Maggy heard familiar voices, she got up from the floor and looked through the curtains covering the window. Among the men outside, she saw her cousin's husband and students she knew from the college in Rusengo. Grabbing Juliette, she went out to meet them, thinking, as she had two days earlier, that she could intervene to stop the impending violence. Before she left the building, she locked the door to the great hall, where many of the people were hiding.

Outside, she confronted the men leading the mob. They demanded that she open the door. When she refused, one of them slapped her; others forced the door open. Maggy tried to negotiate, but they were undeterred. "You and your ideas. We'll burn everything; we'll show you." They proceeded to splash gasoline throughout the great hall and then set the building on fire. Maggy continued to plead and protest, but to these Tutsi men, some of whom were her relatives, the fact that she was seeking to protect Hutu made her a traitor.

Yelling at her insolence, her cousin's husband threatened to kill her. She dared him. "I'll haunt you to the end of your days." He leveled his rifle at her chest but didn't pull the trigger. Instead, he ripped off her clothes, bound her to a nearby chair, and started to beat her. All the while, Maggy kept up her dare. "Beat me, kill me, and I'll come for you in the night."

By this time, the building was on fire and people were fleeing through the single exit to escape the flames and smoke. "Some people came out on fire." Then the killers separated Hutu from Tutsi, and the Tutsi ran away. "They abandoned me," Maggy says.

Some of the Hutu were also able to escape unnoticed. "It was chaos. Not everyone was there to kill. Some were just robbers. Some were survivors of Hutu machetes from two days before. They had spent two days without eating and were looking for food, and for alcohol, because they were in despair." Amid this confusion, Maggy, bound to a chair, watched helplessly as those who had come to kill got on with their business. Some of them had guns, but mostly they had clubs, stones, bamboo spears, and machetes.

Because Juliette was a Tutsi, the killers offered to spare her life, but not her husband's. She responded, "I married not a Hutu but the man I love. If you are going to kill my husband, you should kill me too." Then to Maggy, "Please raise Lydia and Lysette like your own children, love them, give them kindness." The two children were there, with their mother and father. Juliette moved to pass them to Maggy, but her arms were bound to the chair.

"Untie her," Juliette demanded. The killers hesitated until Maggy offered them an incentive: "Untie me, and I'll take you to the coffer where the bishop keeps the money." The offer was attractive. One of the men untied Maggy, and Juliette set Lydia on Maggy's lap. Then to her executioners Juliette said, "Kill me." As one of the them swung his machete, Maggy did her best to divert the attention of Lydia and Lysette.

The children of a Hutu father, Lydia and Lysette were not immune from being the next casualties. Maggy had watched as men with weapons of one kind or another had already killed children, and Lydia and Lysette were not the only children now without parents in the compound. No longer bound, Maggy upped the ante of the bargain that had freed her from the chair. She would lead the killers to the money in the bishop's office in exchange for the lives of Lydia, Lysette, and the other children scattered throughout the compound. The men followed her to the office. But that wasn't the end of it.

"I began also to fight in order to take this child or that child away from a killer, saying, 'Take this,' and giving wine or whiskey, or the key to the storeroom, or some little bit of money, and then in the chaos I hid the children."

Maggy says she was tied to the chair for about an hour, until 10:00 a.m. or so, and that her fight to save children lasted until 1:00 or 2:00 p.m. At one point, she entered the burning building, "until I could no longer stand the heat." The fire became her reference for time. "I can remember, because the fire stopped about 3:00 p.m." She also remembers that after helping children hide, she turned her attention to helping a priest who was trying to save documents from the fire.

Sometime around 3:00 p.m., the killing stopped, the killers departed, and Maggy began looking for the children she had sent into hiding, as well as for her own, whom she had not seen since she left the building hours earlier. When she and Juliette had stepped outside, Chloé was still in her pajamas preparing breakfast. When Maggy couldn't find Chloé or any of her own children among all the bodies strewn around the garden, she panicked.

Distraught, she went into the nearby chapel and unloaded her emotions on God: "My mother lied to me. She told me you were love, but where is love in what I have just witnessed? Where is love in being spared death, in being the one who had to watch everyone else being killed? Where is love in the loss of my own children?"

As she continued railing against God in this way, she heard Chloé's voice from the sacristy. "Mama, we are here. We're alive." Somehow when everyone had scattered in the morning, Chloé had taken her six younger siblings and made it into the chapel, where she'd found a hiding place among the priests' vestments.

Later Chloé described what it was like to be huddled in the sacristy while all the killing was going on outside in the garden. "I heard gun shots. I heard people being killed. I heard wounded people screaming. I also heard Maggy fighting. It wasn't until about 1:00 p.m. that the gunfire stopped. By then, I could no longer hear Maggy, and I thought she was dead."[20]

"When I found my children," Maggy says, "immediately I understood how sublime my vocation was." At sixteen, she had set a course to become a teacher because of what she had experienced during a genocide. As a young teacher of twenty-three, she had adopted a Hutu child who had lost her father to that same event. At twenty-four, she was fired for using her classroom to challenge the Tutsi-led government's discrimination against Hutu. She had then approached Archbishop Ruhuna with her vision for a new generation in Burundi. Now Maggy was the survivor of an ethnically charged massacre of Hutu at the hands of Tutsi, which was revenge for a massacre of Tutsi at the hands of Hutu. And God had spared not only Maggy but her seven Hutu and Tutsi children. "Oh, God, how strange that I discovered my vocation among atrocities."

~

For hours everything had been loud and chaotic and confused. Now chaos gave way to calm as Maggy, on her knees in the chapel in front of the tabernacle that held the Eucharist, apologized to God for misunderstanding his love. Were this a movie, the camera would linger on the scene, a subtle foreshadowing of a life to come. "The Eucharist," Maggy says, "is the source of my true courage. I will never have the same strength as I had in that moment."

After the brief calm, more confusion and fear followed. "We cried together, and then we went out of the little chapel. I showed them the bodies and said, 'Where can we go?' Fabrice, who was five, said, 'But we can go to the German.'" Maggy had adopted Fabrice when he was abandoned as a baby. "He was very clever," Maggy says. She considered his suggestion. "You know, Fabrice, if we go from here to there, they will kill us."

But then Fabrice helped Maggy hatch a plan. She would write a note to Martin Novak, a German aid worker who had a house not far away, and Fabrice would go alone with the note. Meanwhile, Maggy—surrounded by thirty-one children and, but for a T-shirt and a wrap made from curtains, still mostly naked—was worried the killers would come back. "If they find us here, they will kill us." Lysette, three-and-a-half years old, suggested they move to the cemetery. "Hutu and Tutsi are together there."

The cemetery wasn't far, but getting there took time. They traveled with caution, avoiding streets as much as possible, moving through the bush, taking advantage of the coming dusk. Martin found them there about half past six. He and Maggy then returned to the bishop's compound and did their best to cover up the bodies—to hide them, fearing that the perpetrators would come back and make the bodies disappear. It's unclear whether Maggy recovered Juliette's head at this point, or if she had taken it with her to the cemetery. I have never pressed Maggy for that detail.

I did query her once about this part of the story, long after hearing it for the first time, because I had convinced myself that it had come from my dreams and not from Maggy. Sure that I was importing fiction into her story, I asked Maggy if she had really taken Juliette's head with her when she left the scene of the massacre. "Yes, because I couldn't leave her for the dogs." She added that during the night in Martin's house she had hidden the head from three-year-old Lysette, who kept trying to touch it. "I see that you have the head of my mom." It was in response to my query on this occasion that Maggy told me about using the altar cloth from the chapel as a burial shroud for Juliette.

A few days after Martin had rescued Maggy and the children from the cemetery, his organization pulled him out of Burundi. He worked for GTZ, the development arm of the German government, and Germany concluded that Ruyigi had become too dangerous for Martin to stay. GTZ did, however, continue to pay rent for the house so that Maggy and a growing number of orphans could continue to live there. Of these early days, Maggy says, "I was the only adult with the children. Life was hard. I had no money. Sometimes I had to lie and steal to secure food for all the children."

Things took a dramatic turn in mid-May 1994 because of two overlapping events: GTZ pulled out of Burundi completely, and children started arriving to escape the genocide next door in Rwanda—then entering its sixth week—and were overrunning Maggy's ability to house them in Martin's compound. "Suddenly we were more than one hundred children, because of the genocide in Rwanda, and when GTZ pulled out, I had no help, no other aid. It was dangerous because I had to leave Martin's compound, and I had nowhere to go."

That's when Maggy asked the bishop if it would be possible for her to move with the children to an old school building that belonged to the diocese. He agreed. "It was abandoned—even corpses were there. We began to clean up. All the glass was broken from the windows, and it smelled, but we cleaned, put cardboard on the windows, and moved in. We had no choice, because all the children were living in tents I had acquired from UNICEF, and more children were coming every day."

The move into the school in May 1994 coincided with Maggy's creation of Maison Shalom, a formal acknowledgment that Maggy was now in the business of caring for Burundi's abandoned children. The need was by no means limited to Ruyigi, and in February 1995 Maggy opened another orphan center in the nearby community of Butezi. "Many children had died there," she says. "And the Italian volunteers who had lived there for a long time and knew me came and asked, 'Can you open another center?' They owned some abandoned houses. Again, I put life where there had been death. We called it Casa della Pace."

Six months later, Maggy opened a third center, in Gisuru, near the border with Tanzania. "I remember the date," she says. "It was August 15, the feast of the Assumption of Mary. There were many Hutu near the border with no help. Nobody wanted to go there because it was dangerous. I didn't want to work only with Tutsi victims, because I wanted reconciliation. In Gisuru, I started a center not only for children but for mothers who must give birth in the bush with no access to medical care. I called it Oasis de Paix. You see, Casa della Pace, Oasis de Paix, Maison Shalom, they are all the same."

As Maggy's work expanded with more centers and more children, she wasn't counting, but the numbers would eventually rise into the tens of thousands.

～

When Maggy tells her story, she doesn't sort out dates; it's as if everything is happening at once. When I was first piecing things together, I spent considerable time trying to develop an accurate chronology, especially of the first few years. I never really gave up pushing for a timeline, but I learned that Maggy's story resists precise chronology.

A good example is a story Maggy tells about an incident in Bujumbura. "We had no hospital in Ruyigi, and I had many children who needed medical care. I would travel with them to Bujumbura, four hours away. We had nowhere to sleep, and I had no money for a hotel, so we would sleep on the street, even though it wasn't safe. One night, I was sleeping with street kids under a tree, with my children who needed medical care, when a man showed up to bring bread to the street kids. They knew him and called out, 'Henri, the mother from Ruyigi is with us, she's also under the tree.'"

Henri, Maggy explains, was the chief of Belgium's ministry of Federal Public Service in Burundi, the arm of the Belgian government that included its Corporation for Development. Henri had made a habit of bringing bread to the street children in the evenings. He knew Maggy from before the war, she says, when she was "very chic." When he saw her with the street kids, he didn't recognize her. "He said, 'Maggy, is it you?' And I said, 'Yes, Henri. My people betrayed me. But I don't want to betray them.' He cried, and he took me with my children to a house in Bujumbura that belonged to Belgium; later, he gave me that house and three others for my base in Bujumbura."

The chronology Maggy offers for that story is simply, "It was during the war." Of course, it would be possible to track down dates, in part because the rest of the story includes events three years later, when the government of Burundi took the houses away from Maggy, and Belgium threatened a cut in their development aid. The result was government funding for Maggy to buy land and build a center in Bujumbura. If I had pressed Maggy for dates, she would have produced them; but by the time she told me that story, I had long since given up trying to make her life unfold along a timeline.

Some dates, however, simply stand out in Maggy's memory, so much so that she leads with them. October 24, 1993, of course, is one such date, and so is May 28, 1996. On that day, Hutu rebels attacked a camp of internally displaced Tutsi in Butezi, killing forty-nine people, mostly women and children.[21]

Only ten miles from Ruyigi, Butezi was home to Casa della Pace. Maggy had heard that rebels were planning to attack the

Tutsi camp and alerted the regional military commander. "You must send many soldiers." When she heard of the massacre, she made the short trip to Butezi to see what had happened. Along the way, soldiers stopped her at a checkpoint because roads were closed to civilian travel. They told her to return to Ruyigi. She insisted on continuing to Butezi. "Everyone has their own job," she responded. "Weapons and death are yours. It's up to me to rescue and heal." The soldiers let her pass, and she made her way to Butezi. "I went to see them. All those bodies."

It turned out that the government had not sent many soldiers to respond to the request. "Maybe thirty," Maggy says. She learned later that the soldiers had not tried to stop the killers but had given them a free run of the camp. The Tutsi military, Maggy explains, didn't care about Tutsi in the camps. "They wanted to come back to power, to show the international community that Hutu rebels are cruel, that they must not negotiate with them. Again they killed so many people. So many mothers. I found their bodies. Again, I buried them in a mass grave. And I took many children, mutilated children without moms."

Caught up in an all-too-familiar scene, Maggy was overwhelmed. By the time she returned to Ruyigi a few days later, it was clear something was wrong. She had trouble breathing. She lost her voice. She couldn't speak. She went to a doctor, thinking she was having an asthma attack and that she needed an inhaler. "It's not asthma," he told her. "You have another problem. Something an inhaler won't fix."

Sometimes it seems as if Maggy has hyperthymesia—excessive autobiographical memory. Her storytelling resists exact chronology, but it's full of precision and detail. It's also oddly selective. I had heard Maggy tell her story many times before I heard about Butezi and her subsequent breakdown. When I did hear this part of her story, I couldn't quite make sense of it, so I pressed.

"In 1996, when you lost your voice, can you describe that? What happened?" She explained: "I didn't take time to pray. For three years you are there. Surrounding you, you see no compassion, and you want to fight. Then the rebels told me to leave—to take the children because they will attack. But I didn't believe they could kill so many people again. And I told the military, the army, to protect the people in Butezi. I lost my voice because again they betrayed me."

Again is a reference to October 1993, when she also tried to intervene to stop a massacre and was instead beaten and bound and made to watch as some of her own relatives took part in killing seventy-two people. When standing amid the dead and wounded in Butezi, she says, "I wanted to do something." The problem she faced was that since 1993 she *had* been doing something—she had been throwing her entire being into creating orphan centers and saving children, yet here she was nearly three years later gathering up more newly orphaned children from the scene of a massacre that left all their mothers dead.

Unable to function, Maggy sought refuge in a Carmelite monastery in Musongati, twenty miles southwest of Ruyigi. Until that time she had neither prayed nor cried, not really, after the events of 1993. She had been too busy. Now she did both. "I stopped. I was alone. The nuns brought me food. I mourned. I prayed. I began to cry and cry. I went to chapel and mourned for my family. I read my Bible. I reconciled with myself and my story." At first Maggy prayed for understanding, to make sense of the human capacity for cruelty, and then, when that remained a mystery, she prayed simply for the ability to go on.

She remained in silence at the monastery for a month, until she found a new resolve. It came in two forms. On one hand, "I abandoned myself to the hand of God." On the other, "Nobody can lie to me again. I will never again be naive."

Because Maggy leads with love and compassion, it's easy to miss that a visceral reaction to betrayal is one of her driving forces—the influence of her grandfather at work. If, as Maggy says, she is the product of her mother and her grandfather, then it was her month in the monastery following the events at Butezi that, like a master welder joining dissimilar metals, fused these two different influences into a single source of strength.

Maggy admits that until the breakdown that landed her in the monastery, she had been consumed by anger. "You want to fight" she says. When a Tutsi priest ridiculed her because she appeared more upset by the deaths of Hutu than by the loss of more than sixty family members, she said to him, "Hell will not be hot enough for you." When a soldier called her children snakes, she went after him. When at Mass one day she saw a man walking up for communion wearing the clothes of Cyprian, Juliette's husband, she lost it. The priest had to intervene. "Maggy, now you come to church to beat people?" She replied, "Yes, even you I will beat." Reflecting on this time, Maggy says, "I was horrible. Even with God I was violent. I was so angry with God that sometimes in front of the tabernacle I would tell God that if I could beat him I would."

Maggy's time in the monastery was one of conversion. "I discovered that if I accepted in my heart that God is God, that God is powerful, that God is love and tenderness, that God forgives even all this, then I could go on." That last bit she means quite literally. "On many occasions, if it weren't for my faith, I would have killed myself." After the monastery, she says, "I decided to turn the page, to write new pages with children. The children taught me so many things. It's in their eyes that I saw hope and light, and it was the children who showed me how I must love them."

~

In a life that resists precise chronology, it's hard to pin down the exact dates Maggy spent in the monastery. She stayed in Butezi long enough to help bury bodies. She tended to wounded children. And when she returned to Ruyigi, she took the time to go to a doctor. It's likely that June was well underway when she arrived at the monastery. By her account she was still in the monastery on July 20. She remembers the date because that's when what had happened in Butezi was repeated twenty miles away in Bugendana, on a much larger scale.

Witnesses reported that more than a thousand Hutu—armed with guns, machetes, spears, and clubs—overran the twelve soldiers defending the camp of nearly two thousand people and went on a killing spree, throwing incendiary grenades into buildings and hunting down screaming women and children. Survivors said that the killers were singing and dancing while beating the children to death with clubs and asking mothers for money before telling them it was their turn to die. The massacre left 320 people dead, mostly women and children.[22] Or, at least, that's how many bodies were buried in a mass grave on July 23. In this instance, Maggy was not there to help.

The Bugendana attack was a Hutu response to a string of mass killings that had taken place in June at the hands of the Tutsi-led military. On June 12, Tutsi soldiers killed 111 Hutu in Mutambu. On June 28, they rounded up 500 Hutu in Nyeshenza, marched them out of town, and then shot or stabbed them to death. In addition to Hutu and Tutsi trading massacres, three staff of the International Committee of the Red Cross were killed in an ambush on June 4, forcing the ICRC to suspend its activities in the country. The Red Cross didn't return to Burundi until 1999. Some commentators at the time described Burundi as "Rwanda, but in slow motion."[23] This is the world Maggy stepped into when she left the monastery. The capstone event for Maggy came in early September when Archbishop Ruhuna, the man who had helped Maggy find her way after she was fired from her first teaching job, was killed in an ambush.[24]

Speaking of moving back into a landscape of such violence after her experience in the monastery, Maggy says, "I was a new person. I began to dream good things for my children. They began to say, 'Oh, when I finish my studies, I will buy a jet, a private jet for you.' And I would say to them, 'I will build schools for you, and a cinema and a swimming pool, and we will have our restaurant, and a good hospital for children."

Pressing for chronology, I ask, "So all that was coming pretty fast in your imagination, even in 1996, after the monastery?" Maggy replies, "Yes, I began to meet ministers in the government, to go to visit rebels, and to say to both, 'Stop the killing. You will see . . .'" Maggy doesn't finish the sentence. Instead, she jumps to another thought, also incomplete, something to do with refusing to accept nutrition-deficient, genetically modified corn from the World Food Programme and selling WFP six hundred tons of rice from Maison Shalom's organic farms. I found out later that the refusal took place in 2004 and the sale in 2013; but in another example of the collapse of chronology, these events sat right next to the cinema and the swimming pool in Maggy's mind.

Following Maggy's segue into farming, I press again for the origins of what seemed to be a new imagination. "You saw all of that even in 1996?" As if finishing the sentence "You will see . . ." Maggy replies, "Yes. Since that time, I wanted Burundi to become a paradise."

That was a conversation I had with Maggy in 2015, when I was trying to figure out the precise chronology of what she sometimes refers to as her "inventions." I had put a big sheet of poster paper on the table in front of us so that I could construct a chronology one invention at a time. "Every morning," Maggy says, "we invent how to live with dignity." I wanted to move from morning to morning and track the origins of her inventions. What I learned as the poster paper filled up with ink from a Sharpie is that invention isn't linear. It's not as if you imagine something one day and produce it the next.

In 1996, Maggy began to imagine Burundi as a paradise, but it took years for her to invent the things that her imagination envisioned. It also may be that Maggy was little help with chronology because her vision is panoptic: whether looking ahead or looking back, she sees everything at once. The exceptions stand out: the events of October 24, 1993, of May 28, 1996, and of April 17, 2003. Maggy doesn't carry the latter date around in her head like the other two. I've had to track it down.[25] But what happened on that day is no less significant. That was the day Maggy celebrated the opening of La Cité des Anges.

~

The inauguration of the City of Angels, a small campus still under construction in April 2003, marked the culmination of Maggy's post-conversion, imaginative response to a world in which the violence of war and terror had become the norm. After the intense months of 1996, violence remained a constant if inconsistent presence in and around Ruyigi. For the most part, it waxed and waned in time with government responses to rebel movements in and out of base camps in nearby Tanzania. The possibility of a significant de-escalation first arose in August 2000 when the government and seventeen political parties and armed groups vying for power signed a peace agreement that included a detailed three-year plan for the end of the war. The catch was that the most significant rebel group, the one that five years later would produce the first president of a new government, refused to sign, leaving things in Ruyigi in early 2003 much as they had been in 1996.[26]

Between January and April 2003, fighting in and around Ruyigi led to the deaths of more than four hundred civilians and the displacement of tens of thousands. On two days in

January alone, government forces looted and burned hundreds of homes, killed dozens of civilians, including children, and raped women and girls—all because they suspected civilians of collaborating with rebels. These forces also denied humanitarian aid agencies access to the population displaced by fighting. Meanwhile, the rebels were also raping women and girls, stealing from villages, extorting civilians, and forcibly recruiting child soldiers.[27]

Speaking to an interlocutor at the end of 2003, Maggy said: "Do you remember the month of April? We couldn't go even twenty kilometers outside town. If we wanted to travel, we couldn't leave Ruyigi before 9:00 a.m., and we had to be back by 4:00. There were shells falling on the town of Ruyigi, and we were stuck. It was total insecurity in our region."[28]

That insecurity was the immediate backdrop of the inauguration of the City of Angels. "This night they attacked," Maggy says, adding "boom" for emphasis. What she describes started early in the morning, about 1:00 a.m., when fierce fighting broke out between government soldiers and rebels near Ruyigi. Artillery exchanges knocked out several of the towers in the transmission lines that brought electricity, leaving the town without power. Maggy was undeterred, and the ceremony she had planned proceeded despite the nearby fighting and the lack of electricity.

Attending the inauguration were the ambassador of Belgium, emissaries from the French embassy, UNICEF's country director, the provincial governor of Ruyigi, various other local dignitaries, and as many people from the community as could fit alongside dozens and dozens of Maggy's children inside the compound of the small campus. The main attraction was Le Cinéma des Anges, the only movie theater in a country of six million people other than one in Bujumbura. The celebration was to include the screening of the first films in the new theater, but the power outage made that impossible.

Instead, the ceremony narrowed to a ribbon-cutting, followed by speeches, and then music and dancing and tours.

The welcome speech fell to one of the children Maggy had taken in during those first few months when she was living in Martin Novak's house and taking in orphans. Justine was only nine years old in October 1993 when a neighbor set the family's house on fire, killed her parents and her sister, and left her wounded with machete blows to the head. That's how she ended up with Maggy. Now she was a young woman of eighteen living back in her village in the house of her birth. The man who had killed her parents and sister still lived next door. He and Justine had reconciled. Indeed, he had helped her rebuild the home he had destroyed. Sometime later, she would care for him as he was dying.

To those who knew her story, Justine's welcome speech would not have been a surprise: "Dear parents, brothers and sisters, welcome to our home. The Cinema of Angels will be a challenge to war and a challenge to AIDS, a return to hope, and a place of reunion and conviviality between two ethnic groups in conflict."[29]

∼

Moving Justine from an orphan center to her home village was an early experiment in what would become another of Maggy's inventions, one she was scaling up during the same years she was creating the City of Angels. She called this invention *Fratrie*—French for "siblings." The key was returning orphans to their own villages and, with the help of the community, building them houses, sometimes on the land of their parents, as with Justine. When possible, children from the same biological family made up the core of each house. In houses where the older children were mature enough to function as elders and create a stable family, Maison Shalom provided little outside supervision. In houses where the children were younger or had special needs of some kind, Maison Shalom assigned a woman to check in regularly and sometimes to spend the night. Children with no biological siblings were adopted into an existing house.

Significantly, Maison Shalom conveyed the title of each house to the elder children. They could sell the house or pass it down in keeping with traditional Burundian practice. In time it became routine, Maggy says, for children who were moving out of the house for a job or to be married to give the house away to other children as an act of gratitude for what they themselves had received.

On their face, the *Fratrie* seemed to owe much to Hermann Gmeiner and SOS Children's Villages, like the one where Maggy taught in the 1980s. Curious about the influence, I queried Maggy in a WhatsApp text message, "When you started moving children into houses did you have SOS Children's Villages in mind as a model?" When trying to clarify various details in Maggy's story, texting her had become part of my method of inquiry. Usually she would text back within a day or so; in this case, I got an immediate phone call. She was worried that I suggested a connection to Gmeiner's model and wanted to make sure I understood that it was an influence only in an entirely negative sense. "What I was doing was the opposite of the bad experience I had when teaching in the SOS Children's Village."

Maggy was so opposed to Gmeiner's model that on one occasion she traveled to the headquarters of SOS Children's Villages in Austria to make her case against the model as it was playing out in Africa. Gmeiner himself was dead—he died in 1986—and Maggy addressed his successors. She told them that although in principle Gmeiner's model privileged keeping children from the same biological family together, in practice unrelated teenagers were often placed in the same house, which led to a lot of teenage pregnancies.

The model was also problematic because oversight for each house excluded family members and fell instead to a female employee of SOS Children's Villages who functioned as a "mother." Even more, the model failed because it created dependency by treating the children like wards, providing them with everything they needed until they moved away when they turned eighteen. "And where were they to go?" Maggy asked. "By the time they were forced to leave, they had become entirely dependent on the village." With a sense of irony, she added, "Of course, we were obliged to welcome them into Maison Shalom."

Stark differences between Maggy's model and Gmeiner's (at least as he conceived of it originally) are apparent in the two basic criteria Gmeiner put in place for accepting orphans into a village: first, a child "must be healthy enough, physically and emotionally, to live in a family without receiving special attention," and, second, "children who might be cared for by relatives or friends are not accepted." Maggy took in all children, regardless of their physical or emotional condition, and the ideal house was one supervised by a relative, since the aim was to preserve the biological family when possible.

There is one notable similarity, beyond the general idea of putting children in houses instead of orphanages and keeping siblings together when possible. Of his houses Gmeiner said, "The idea of a children's village began to grow in my mind. Nothing in this village would be gray. Gray is the color of prisons and reformatories. There would be bright cheerful colors." When we toured Ruyigi in 2009, Maggy made a point of telling us we would know her children's houses when we saw them because they would be the ones with flowers in the yard.[30]

The negative example of Gmeiner's model was in the background, but the proximate cause for the invention of the *Fratrie* was something that happened one day when a woman stopped Maggy at Mass: "I want you to hear what my son just said to me." Turning to her son, she said, "Go ahead. Tell Maggy." The boy spoke. "I asked mama when she would die so I could come live with you." Maggy was horrified. Amid war, poverty, and the AIDS epidemic, the children in Maison Shalom's orphan centers were better off than children in the villages. Maggy saw immediately that her model of caring for orphans was flawed.

"Children belong to the community, to the village, not to my centers." Maison Shalom had always conducted searches for the village of a child's origin—a kind of proactive lost and found. "We worked with parishes and the local administration to find the family of origin, even when there was no one left. We wanted to show children where they were born. Even when there was no one to welcome them." The *Fratrie* extended that practice, and it did so in part because of what Maggy had learned from her early experiment with Justine.

When Maggy proposed to Justine that Maison Shalom return her to the village and rebuild the house of her parents, Justine objected. "No, I think we will call the man who killed my parents and show him the burned house." Maggy replied, in disbelief, "We call this killer?" Justine insisted, "Yes, of course, because I want to rebuild first the heart not the house. I will tell him what he must do for us to make reconciliation. If I hate him, I can't live." Maggy sometimes ends Justine's story by describing what she learned from children like Justine. "Forgiveness is the key to life. Hatred in your heart will kill you. Without forgiveness, there is no future. This is what the children taught me. They taught me how to forgive. Forgiveness is a process; it was not easy for me."

About the time Maggy was learning the lesson of forgiveness from Justine, she had the opportunity to put it into practice. The man who had killed two of her aunts—burning them to death—was in prison. She went to visit him. "His name was Caspar," she tells me. "The guard didn't want me to see him. 'Maggy, Maggy, he's the killer, the one who killed your aunts. We punished him.' I said, 'You punished him? Then you became killers too. I must see him.' They took me to him. He had been tortured. They had refused to give him food."

Maggy stops to show me a photograph. It's in a French edition of *GEO* magazine, a European version of *National Geographic*. The photograph was part of a story the magazine had done on Maggy in 1997. A young man is sitting on a worn-out mattress on a rickety, rusting bed frame. He is leaning back, his arms bracing him, as a woman works to bend his swollen, scar-covered knee. Except for a wrap around his groin, he is naked, his skeletal frame in full view. The image rivals the worst photographs of Auschwitz survivors. "You see how he is," Maggy says. "I asked if I could bring him to the hospital. They let me. When we got there, he asked me, 'Maggy, why are you doing this?' I said, 'Caspar, a criminal you are, but still you are a child of God. Today, you can be a criminal, but tomorrow you can be a savior.' He looked at me and said, 'Your forgiveness gives me back my humanity.'"

The prison forgot about Caspar, and later Maggy helped him escape to Tanzania. "I told him, 'Please save other people as I taught you.' This was, for me, justice, because in Burundi there was no justice in the tribunals." The journalist who took the photograph didn't understand. "I said to him, 'What would you want, that I kill him and become a criminal like him?' I want to heal." That stark choice between killing and healing echoed something Justine would say later in a speech she gave in 2001, two years before welcoming people to the City of Angels.

The occasion was Maison Shalom's celebration of eighty-five *Fratrie* in Ruyigi. "Maggy gave us love and grace," Justine said. "She was not obliged to do it. We were not part of her family. If I hadn't found her, I myself would have become a killer."[31] It would have been easy, Maggy says, for Maison Shalom to have become a house of rebels, of children waiting to grow old enough to kill the killers of their parents. What Maggy learned from children like Justine was that to love them, "I must change their life and make them like candles among the darkness."

~

The *Fratrie* and the theater that anchored the City of Angels were both essential components of Maggy's candle-making—something not lost on Malick Sene, the country director for UNICEF, who helped fund Le Cinéma des Anges. Malick's decision to lend UNICEF's support to the project was prompted by an encounter he had with Maggy at a conference UNICEF organized in Bujumbura in March 2003. Maggy still remembers the title: *Formation intervenants en faveur des enfants en détresse aiguë* (Training for workers working with children in acute distress).

"They called together all the organizations taking care of sick children, child soldiers, AIDS children, and so on. We met in the most expensive hotel in Bujumbura. Everybody, of course, had a PowerPoint for their projects, asking for a big car, computers, salaries, rent for the office, but nothing for the children. I was there, thinking . . ." The ellipsis is a moment of love becoming an invention, but Maggy skips the details and jumps to what her thinking led her to do. "Before lunch, I left the room. In front of the hotel, there were many street children who had nothing to eat. I said, 'Come, come.' And I brought them to the buffet that had been prepared for lunch, and they ate all the food."

When the conference broke for lunch and attendees found no food, they asked the cook in the kitchen what had happened. She replied, "Maggy said that you were not going to eat, that the food was for the children." When conference organizers chastised Maggy, she responded, "The children in acute distress, the ones who are sick and dying, the ones in the title of this conference, they are right here, but this morning you turned everything into a business."

People were angry. "But it was good," Maggy says, "because the country director of UNICEF came to me and cried and said, 'Forgive me.' When we returned to the conference room, he said to everyone, 'Now I have seen the one we will fund.'" This result of Maggy's ploy with the street children did not endear her to other local organizations seeking UNICEF's money. "They were angry," she says. "They tried to bomb my office in Bujumbura, because they lost the money they were prepared to receive."

Months later when Malick was asked why UNICEF would fund a project as unusual as Maggy's theater, he said, "I have been in Ruyigi several times and seen the desolation. Proximity with Tanzania leads to almost daily battles between soldiers and rebels, making things much darker. To see Maggy who's there, and who . . ." he stutters, searching for words. "We have the impression that she does not live in her surroundings. She tries to see things differently, to see things that aren't dark, that aren't sad, even though all around there is sadness, there is unhappiness. In terms of health centers, we have built some. In terms of schools, we have done a lot. A lot has been done. But what is missing now is the cement to bind this together, to open hearts. I think the Cinema of Angels is the answer. We don't live on bread and water alone."[32]

At the inauguration of the City of Angels, Le Cinéma des Anges was the primary evidence of Maggy's knack for seeing things differently, but for those paying attention something else was in the works. A few steps away from the theater, a small army of workers was digging a hole in the ground. Maggy was constructing a swimming pool—like the theater, the only one in the country outside Bujumbura. In April 2003, the pool wasn't finished; it was just a rectangular hole in Ruyigi's red clay, growing deeper by the day. By the end of the year, however, it was an aqua-colored wonder surrounded by a skirt of red tile with a shining chrome ladder at each end.

Asked to explain the pool, Maggy says:

For those people who suffered so much in war I built a swimming pool. We were not just there to give out food and clothes but to distribute dignity and hope. All the time, my children were afraid. They had no place to play. They had become victims. All children, not just orphans. I wanted to give them dignity. When I looked around, I saw that there was no dialogue between the military and the rebels, between Tutsi and Hutu. I wanted to act, to show them that they can come and swim together. I even invited the rebels. I told them, "You have a right to play. You must not always be thinking about killing your enemies."

Maggy invited government soldiers and rebels to the theater as well, where fixed to the door was a red circle with a slash across the middle painted on top of the black silhouette of an AK-47. "I saw that Hutu and Tutsi couldn't talk to each other. And so I said, 'Tomorrow another war will begin because people are not together. How can I give them the opportunity to dream?' In town I saw fear. They were all so anxious. They had no idea what was happening outside Burundi. I built a cinema so they could talk together, watch a movie together, heal each other, leave the trauma behind."

The goal of showing films to children was the same. "We are going to offer children an image, an image that is not of war, an image that is not of AIDS, of death, but an image of hope. You see what we are going through in our region of Ruyigi, with the shells we launch, with the war, with displaced people, people who are injured. There have to be people who believe in reconciliation."

~

When electricity was restored two days after the inauguration of the City of Angels, the first film shown for adults in the theater was *Romeo and Juliet*. Interestingly, this is also the first film Maggy saw—at the country's only theater, in Bujumbura, when she was fourteen. Shakespeare's famous tragedy opens with the words, "Two households, both alike in dignity, in fair Verona, where we lay our scene, from ancient grudge break to new mutiny, where civil blood makes civil hands unclean."

The message was not lost on those in attendance, some of whom were young men and women who had come to Maison Shalom as children. Of the film, one of these young Burundians said, "In this movie, there was a young girl named Juliet, and a young man named Romeo. Juliet's parents and Romeo's parents didn't get along, but, fortunately, these young people loved each other, so much so that they loved each other until they died to overcome the faults of their parents. Watching this movie, I had a moral lesson that inspired me: love has no barriers, no borders, so we can marry a girl from the enemy family."[33]

To feel the full force of those words is to place them in context. About a year before Maggy started working on the theater, Chloé had come back to Burundi after five years of medical school in Italy. She started working as a physician for Maison Shalom. "We receive children of all ethnicities here, and everywhere you go, whether you are Hutu or Tutsi, you are spat upon. If you go to the Hutu, you are accused of having taken in Tutsi children. If you go to a Tutsi house, you are accused of taking in Hutu children. Yet Maggy is a Tutsi, and I am a Hutu, and we share everything. The children here are aware of their ethnicity, and yet they live together without any problems. This is the Burundi of tomorrow." The moral lesson of Romeo and Juliet for the young adults who came to Maison Shalom as children was not simply that they could marry anyone they wanted to, but that the Burundi of tomorrow rested on a love that was more powerful than death.

The first film Maggy showed the young children was *Kirikou and the Sorceress*, an animated film based on West African folktales. Set in a West African village, the plot revolves around a boy named Kirikou, who saved his village from an evil sorceress. All the men in the village except one had disappeared, and it was rumored that she had eaten them. When the boy learned from his grandfather that the sorceress was not evil but afflicted by a poisoned thorn, the boy found a way to trick her and remove the thorn, after which the missing men returned, and the village was restored to health.

Although carrying a subtler message than *Romeo and Juliet*, the film certainly created possibilities for giving Maggy's younger charges a new imagination for how to think about their own lives in Burundi. Over time, film choice created controversy because Maggy refused to show action films that traded on gratuitous violence, despite the fact that, some people argued, that would have been a better economic model, because more people would pay to see such movies.

~

To complete the City of Angels, Maggy made additions. After the theater and the swimming pool came a library and vocational training for tailors and beauticians. Next door, in 2005, she created Le Garage des Anges, where former child soldiers could take a step toward peace and become car mechanics. Maggy rattles off the sequence of causes and effects that created the City of Angels and the other inventions of Maison Shalom:

> People came in the evenings to watch films. I saw that they began to stop killing, so I said, "Oh, I can also put in a library." Then they came to read, and I said, "I see that they need internet," so I built a cybercafé to give them a window on the world, because they were thinking only

about war. Then I put in a reception hall for weddings, and they had their pictures taken near the pool. Then I saw that women needed nice clothes, and also their hair done—so I opened a tailor shop and a beauty salon. Then I paid the rebels to give me child soldiers, but I needed something for them to do, so nearby I built a mechanics garage to fix cars. Still, there was so much unemployment, so I said, "Oh, I can make a little restaurant." I created a restaurant, and a bakery, for all the young people to come to after swimming. And I talked with them, "What can you do?" Some said, "I can learn to sew." Others, "I can learn to cook." So I started vocational training. Then I also built a guest house where visitors could stay. It is like that.

It is like that is one of Maggy's favorite phrases. She uses it often at the end of such summaries of her life and work, a punctuated pause that allows her to catch her breath and gather her thoughts. It's a verbal ellipsis standing in for all the things she could go on to say were there time to do so.

Once I was with Maggy around a dinner table with others when she was telling the story about the time Henri found her sleeping with street children and proceeded to give her four houses in Bujumbura. She ended the story with "It is like that," and I said to the others at the table, "With Maggy, it is always like that." Maggy responded, "Yes. Always providence, like the widow of Zarephath."

The reference was to a biblical story in 1 Kings 17 about God providing food for the prophet Elijah after sending him into hiding during a time of drought. "You will drink from the brook, and I have directed the ravens to supply you with food." When the stream dries up and Elijah needs to move, God sends new instructions. "Go now to Zarephath, which belongs to Sidon, and live there, for I have commanded a widow there to feed you." Elijah finds the widow, but she has only a small amount of food and is dying of starvation. "I have nothing baked, only a handful of meal in a jar and a little oil in a jug; I am now gathering a couple of sticks so that I may go home and prepare it for myself and my son, that we may eat it and die."

Elijah tells the widow to bake what she can and feed him first. "Do not be afraid. For thus says the Lord the God of Israel: 'The jar of meal will not be emptied and the jug of oil will not fail until the day that the Lord sends rain on the earth.' She went and did as Elijah said, so that she as well as he and her household ate for many days. The jar of meal was not emptied, neither did the jug of oil fail." Following her reference to this story, Maggy said, "This is the experience of my life. Never be afraid. God will always feed you. And when he doesn't, trust that he will."

~

In the chronology of Maggy's post-conversion inventions, it's hard to pinpoint exactly when the idea for La Cité des Anges came to be, but it's clear that first intimations surfaced one night in Paris, sometime in late 2000. By then, trips to Paris or elsewhere in Europe had become common for Maggy. Sometimes she traveled for conferences, sometimes to seek medical care for severely wounded children, sometimes to find funding for Maison Shalom. On this occasion, she was in Paris attending a symposium on HIV/AIDS, where she met up with Thierry Nutchey, a French writer and filmmaker. Maggy had met Thierry in Burundi in 1999, when he was there for three months to supervise the shooting of a series of short documentaries focusing on peace, reconciliation, and the reconstruction of a war-torn country.

Having read somewhere that Thierry was involved in Le Cinéma des Anges, I reached out to see what he might be able to add to what I had learned from Maggy about the origins of the theater. It was not my habit to chase down Maggy's friends or acquaintances for details about her story. I decided early on to leave that to some future biographer. Thierry became an exception, however, because I simply could not fathom how it came to be that Maggy decided to build a movie theater in rural Burundi in the middle of a war.

Thierry fleshed out the story, starting with how he first met Maggy. "One of the films I supervised in 1999," he explained, "featured Maggy's work in Ruyigi, where famine was raging and waves of rebels were moving through from neighboring Tanzania—where they had set up their rear bases in refugee camps. At the time, Ruyigi was dangerous and cut off from everything, and Maggy's situational awareness and courage struck me immediately. We talked a lot and got on well and, strengthened by this friendship and overwhelmed by the situation of the children and of Ruyigi, I proposed that I return the following year—2000—to film a full-length documentary. That film became *L'armée des anges*."[34]

To make the documentary, Thierry had filmed the funerals and burials of infants who had died from AIDS in Ruyigi. He saw firsthand the toll that caring for those with AIDS was taking on Maggy and her work. When he met Maggy that evening in Paris, knowing she had spent a long day talking about the havoc AIDS was wreaking in Burundi, he decided to invite her to accompany him to a movie, "just to give her a change of mind." Maggy accepted the invitation, saying that it had been fifteen years since she had been to Burundi's lone theater—the Cameo in Bujumbura—to see a movie.

The film they watched was Wong Kar-wai's *In the Mood for Love*, which earlier that year had premiered to critical acclaim at the Cannes Film Festival. "We saw the film on a large screen," Thierry recalled, "in a beautiful room, and I understood quickly how much Maggy was moved by these images. At the exit, she said to me, in a joking tone, or perhaps already dreaming a little, 'It would be so good if the children of Ruyigi could see such images one day.' I replied, also jokingly, 'Well why not!?'"

Within a short time, this light-hearted conversation turned into a plan. "Two or three days later," Thierry said, "I called her back and we decided to do it. I remember that it took time to get started. We had to design the project and look for funding. I created a small association in France to find funding and equipment. I asked all the professionals and friends around me, and all the material was donated. The seats came from a cinema in France that was closing. When they arrived in Burundi, Maggy's sewing workshop refurbished them. For her part, Maggy acquired the land and some buildings—in ruins—where we built."

That's the origin story of an idea, but it's not yet an account of Maggy's imagination. While Thierry was pulling pieces together in France, Maggy was back in Burundi searching for a place to build a theater. The lot she eventually acquired sat between Ruyigi's soccer stadium and the city's open-air market. It had been the site of a small hotel. "During the war," Maggy explains, "the proprietor lost money, and then the bank took it. It was a waste, a ruin—empty and broken and a dumping ground."

The lot was also right next to an army camp. When Maggy tried to buy the land, the minister of defense said he would not allow it. Maggy went to court and won. Even when she had the title in hand, however, the minister of defense tried to stop her from taking ownership. "You may not go there." Maggy knew the source of his objection: government soldiers were using the site for the secret disposal of the bodies of rebel fighters. That's why Maggy set her sights on this particular lot for the theater. She explains by breaking into French, as she often does when her English falls short of what she wants to say: *Là où a abandonné la haine ou la mort je voulais faire vivre la vie.* English that comes close would be something like: "Where hatred or death left a wasteland, I wanted to create life."

From the start, the City of Angels was just what Justine would say of it later. It was a challenge to war. "I was thinking about how I could break the cycle," Maggy says. "Maybe I could stop the military from killing people because they would not have another place to put the bodies. I didn't want all of Ruyigi to become a cemetery. It was such a wonderful place when I was a child."

Because of the army's objections, it wasn't easy for Maggy to move onto the lot. She started by showing up at night and taking over the lot with singing, dancing, and drumming children—effectively staging a kinetic sit-in. The soldiers in the camp would tell her to go away. She would say, "This is my place." As this grew into a nightly confrontation, people from all over Ruyigi showed up. "They started to make noise," Maggy says. "Let this mother continue. What she's doing, she's doing for us." Finally, the soldiers in the camp gave up, saying, "What can we do with this?"

The first thing Maggy did once she was able to move forward with plans for the theater was to disinter the bodies stashed away on the overgrown lot and to rebury them in the city cemetery. Then she started planning the swimming pool. In the long "it-was-like-that" list of the things Maggy added to the theater to create the City of Angels, the swimming pool came first. She wanted to give the children a place to play. She might have installed slides and swing sets, but her choice of a swimming pool had deeper origins. "As a Christian, I was thinking about how I could clean up the mass grave. I also wanted to clean the town, to purify Ruyigi, every citizen. A swimming pool is symbolic of baptism."

The swimming pool was still under construction when Maggy invited all the dignitaries to gather with her children and the people of Ruyigi to celebrate the completion of the theater. The day Maggy chose for the celebration was April 17, 2003. That date is noteworthy because it was Holy Thursday— the launch of Easter, with its three days of remembrance and a fourth of celebration. In liturgical tradition, Thursday's Mass ends in darkness, to prepare for the crucifixion on Friday. Saturday comes as a pause. Jesus is dead and interred in a tomb. Sunday is the day of resurrection. The traditional Easter celebration takes place with a vigil on Saturday, in the dark after sunset. Celebrants pierce the darkness by lighting a fire outside the church. Parishioners then light candles from the fire and process into a darkened sanctuary.

Out of the same theological imagination that led her to replace a mass grave with a swimming pool, Maggy set her sights on Easter for the public unveiling of the invention she saw as a challenge to war. That the war itself stretched the full inauguration of the City of Angels to align with the flow of Easter liturgies was a fitting accident of circumstance. Because fighting had knocked out power in Ruyigi, tours of the Cinema of Angels on Thursday took place in a darkened theater. By the time power returned and light from the first films flickered in the darkness, it was Saturday.

~

Maggy's war-time projects were not limited to the *Fratrie*, the cinema, and the swimming pool. "*Every* morning," she says, "we invent how to live with dignity." One morning in 2001, the need for another invention emerged. Maison Shalom had received sixteen newborns at a time its centers were already caring for more than 250 infants, many of them at the Oasis de Paix near the Tanzanian border.

Chloé, then about to leave the country for medical school in Italy, remembers the impetus for opening the center in Gisuru. "Fleeing people were trying to reach refugee camps just across the border. Women were dying while fleeing or trying to return to Burundi. Newborn babies were abandoned on the roads or left to their fathers who were unable to feed them."[35] Trying to save infants like these, Maggy opened Oasis de Paix in 1995. Now it was 2001, and the influx of so many newborns on a single day caused Maggy to wonder why sixteen mothers had died. She decided to find out.

"It was dangerous," Maggy says. "I went to see the villages. I slept in the villages. I talked to mothers." A journalist's description of Ruyigi during these years helps puts Maggy's comments in context. "Ruyigi was still a small village with an archaic economy in a war zone, with a sanitary infrastructure lower than the vital minimum, with little food provisions, with an overfilled prison, and with hills devastated by fire. This region was the one most harmed by the civil war. The positions of Burundian rebels in Tanzania obliged them to pass systematically through the area around Ruyigi, where the chaos was intense: raped women, hundreds of dead bodies, destroyed schools, a ravaged health center, and devastated villages."[36] Maggy describes seeing women with no food, no shelter, and no clothes. She saw babies with no milk. She saw men who were drunk, "hardcore," she says.

When she returned from her trip, she asked herself, "What can I do?" The solution seemed clear. "I will build a maternity center." But the idea formed much faster than her ability to enact it. Construction didn't start until 2007. For the location, Maggy chose a site on the leading edge of Nyamutobo Hill, just above town. During the war, the site had been strategic—high ground for artillery batteries. For construction, Maggy enlisted government soldiers. "And in this place where they used to kill people, they themselves built the maternity center." Construction was underway from January to April, and when the center opened a short time later it brought into full view the needs Maggy had encountered in the villages. "So many women came. Very ill. They came, many returning from refugee camps in Tanzania. And then I saw that I must build a hospital. Because I saw the miserable situation of these women."

~

Rema Hospital opened in January 2008, just a few hundred feet away from the maternity center, atop the ruins of Maggy's ancestral village. The hospital came to be because one thing led to another. "It is like that," as Maggy is wont to say. Orphan centers and houses, a swimming pool and movie theater, a mechanics garage, a library, a vocational training school, a restaurant, a bakery, a guest house, a maternity center . . . and then a hospital.

First a maternity ward and a lab. Then a surgery. Then pediatrics, followed by neonatology, and soon, "The hospital was the center of everything. For me, these buildings, this hospital, the plans were in my heart. When the architects came, I said, 'I don't want to build near the street. When people come to the hospital, I want them to feel like we sing in the psalm: "We're going up to Jerusalem."' I told the architects, 'I want a chapel here because the morgue is there, and people will pass this way, because we are not a hospital only.' Maison Shalom is a message: we believe in life. It's life that has the last word."

Rema Hospital was constructed exactly as Maggy envisioned it. The entrance sits a football field away from the street. The natural progression from entrance to exit passes around the wards to the morgue, the building that sits the farthest from the street and anchors the whole complex to the flat top of Nyamutobo Hill. From the morgue the road takes a sharp turn back toward the exit, passing the chapel as the last stop. "From the morgue," Maggy says, "the family and community can bring their loved one here to say farewell and give the gift of life back to God." For Maggy, a morgue without a chapel nearby would be unthinkable.

I noted in the preface that the tour of Rema Hospital Maggy gave me and my colleagues in 2009 was profoundly disorienting, that it was in fact the impetus for me to seek out Maggy and pester her with questions. Especially in the early years, before I had developed a relationship with Maggy and my contact with her was limited, I would sometimes give my questions to others to ask on my behalf. One of these occasions was Maggy's visit to Duke in 2013. She was on campus to receive an honorary degree. A local news anchor had arranged a studio interview for the evening news. He'd never met Maggy before and asked me for questions to guide his interview. I gave him a long list. At the top of the list was a question about the morgue.

I don't remember how I phrased my question, but this is what the news anchor asked Maggy: "Because you have witnessed so much dying, is that why you built such a prominent morgue?"

Yes, because I have seen my brothers and sisters trivialize life. I have seen people taking machetes and—*foompf*—like that . . . In 1993, I saw dogs with the hands of my friends in their mouths. And I said, "I am Christian, I know that human life is sacred. You can't vandalize it. How can I show my brothers, my Burundian brothers and sisters, that life is sacred, that bodies are sacred?" And that is why the morgue is important for the hospital, for me. That is why in the hospital, the morgue is more expensive than pediatrics.

All the people told me I was crazy, but for me it is not a hospital. It is a sacred place. We heal people. Our human vocation is to heal our brothers and sisters. It is a unique vocation. It is not to build stupid things. God gave us Eden. And now we can rebuild, even in our hearts, the Garden. You see, everybody comes to the hospital.

When I saw Rema Hospital in 2009, it was clearly the crowning achievement of Maison Shalom and of everything Maggy had created up to that point. It took me years to figure out the details, but even in that moment it was clear that these buildings, in every respect recognizable as a hospital, were also more than that. Or, rather, they were a hospital of an entirely different sort, one constructed around a morgue.

I didn't fully understand the impactful novelty of Maggy's design until an American physician approached me after a presentation I had given on Maggy and Rema Hospital. "I've worked in and visited hospitals all over the United States," the physician said, "and the morgue is always in the same place: in the basement near the laundry and the garbage, so that all three can share a loading dock as a requirement of industrial efficiency. Formally speaking, after all, bodies are simply medical waste." Absent his stark contrast between the design of American hospitals and what Maggy had built in Burundi, I had not appreciated the extent to which Rema Hospital was the product of a moral imagination.

"In my hospital," Maggy says, "it's not just that you go to see the doctor and then get medicine and leave. When you enter, there are social workers and psychologists. Beyond that there are baths. And it is beautiful, with flowers. Then when you continue there is a place for massage. Because of the war, the trauma, people are afraid to touch each other. We say, 'We can give you a little massage. Take a break. Sit.' Then we bring oil, and we sing. We put on music for the baby who is there. We heal all trauma . . ." Her words trail off into another "And it is like that."

Although the hospital was the product of one thing leading to another over fifteen years, its true origin rests back in 1996, when Maggy went to Butezi after the massacre there. In the back-and-forth ritual of the civil war, Tutsi soldiers had killed Hutu in the streets of Butezi to avenge the Tutsi deaths in the camp. "I remember I was driving down the street, and I saw so many bodies because the military had killed many people, and I stopped to put those bodies in my car to give them dignity. One of the bodies was a woman with a baby on her back. They had killed the woman with a grenade. When I took the baby, I found that his mouth was gone, but he was still alive."

Maggy took the baby to a Tutsi-run government hospital. She knew they would not care for the baby if they connected him with the recent killing of the Hutu, so she lied and told them that Hutu rebels had thrown a grenade that had injured her baby. "Look," she said, "he lost his mouth and part of his tongue." They asked her the baby's name, and she made up one on the spot: Dieudonné, *Gift from God*. "We can't save your child," the nurses said. "Go over there. In ten minutes, he will die." Maggy offered to give blood or do whatever she needed to do, but they told her to go away.

Maggy responded, "One day I will build a hospital where Hutu, Tutsi, Congolese, and others will come." Then she left with the child she had named Gift from God. He didn't die. For two years Maggy cared for him, sometimes enduring criticism for her attachment. "'You are clinging to Dieudonné,' I was told. It's true that I missed certain meetings dedicated to finding grants, but I held up for two years."[37] Eventually Maggy was able to get Dieudonné to Germany for two reconstructive surgeries. "He is handicapped," Maggy says, "but he lives. This is the challenge of God—that always love takes the last word. And this is my life."

It's noteworthy that Maggy would utter those words when recalling the story of Dieudonné more than twenty-five years later, during a conversation we had in 2022. Lots would happen in her life after she found Dieudonné on the street in Butezi: almost two decades of Burundian inventions; a million-dollar award for social entrepreneurship; assassination attempts; flight and exile; another million-dollar award, this one for awakening humanity; more inventions; an expanding message. All that and more would transpire after Maggy rescued Dieudonné from his mother's back and clung to him for two years, but that's the memory that leads her to say, "And this is my life."

An image comes to mind, one that condenses Maggy's life to its essentials: a woman clinging to a wounded child, a Burundian *Pietà*.

~

Only after many conversations with Maggy did I begin to understand the shape of her life and the mechanics of her imagination. I was helped along by returning to the photographs I took on our tour of Ruyigi in 2009. I kept studying them, like a forensics specialist looking for clues.

The photographs and their time stamps helped me realize that at every turn the tour Maggy gave us of Maison Shalom moved us from one grave site or site of violence and death to the next. Our first stop was the mass-grave-become-swimming-pool; our second stop was the razed-village-become-hospital; our third stop was the mass grave and memorial in the makeshift cemetery near the bishop's compound. Our final stop was a morgue—not Maggy's morgue but the one at the government hospital.

In a strategic move that mimicked what she had done with the swimming pool, the maternity center, and the hospital, Maggy built her house on the lot that had been serving as a dumping ground for medical waste from the government hospital. The ramshackle shack that served as the government morgue stood just off the back corner of the hospital, no more than a hundred feet from Maggy's house. Within a few feet of the morgue, Maggy had constructed a chapel. On our tour, she took us into the chapel and explained why she had built it so close to the morgue.

"They call us when a person or a baby dies. And we go, and we bring the body here, and we pray, and we prepare it for burial." During the war, she said, bodies had become no more than corpses to discard or to step over in the street. What she had learned was that to teach people to care for the living she first had to teach them to care for the dead. That's what she was doing when she was pulling dead bodies into her car and discovered Dieudonné strapped to his mother's back.

At the time, I didn't comprehend Maggy's lesson because I was not conceptually equipped to make sense of it. Only years later, when reading Robert Pogue Harrison's *The Dominion of the Dead*, did I begin to understand what Maggy was saying. Writing about the decline of Rome, Harrison says, "Nothing reveals the spiritual exhaustion of the Romans more than their need to incessantly reproduce and inflate the scene of senseless death. As death began to lose its sanctity, so too did life, leading gradually but inexorably to a lust for the daily spectacle of murder—of animals, gladiators, criminals, or Christians." In words that could have been Maggy's, Harrison adds, "Where the dead are simply dead, the living are in some sense already dead as well."[38]

Harrison delivers his punch line, which precedes his argument, this way: "Let me put forward a premise, to the effect that humanity is not a species; it is a way of being mortal and relating to the dead. As human beings, we are born of the dead, of the regional ground they occupy, of the languages they inhabited, of the worlds they brought into being. To be human means above all to bury."[39] Harrison's premise has a metaphorical component, but he also means for us to take it literally: the practice of burying our dead marks us as distinct among the life forms that have evolved on this planet.

On this note, the city of Çatalhöyük—first inhabited nine thousand years ago in the region that is now southwestern Turkey—is instructive. Beneath the floor of house after house, archaeologists have found the skeletal remains of the dead. Similar burial practices characterized other Neolithic cities, where archaeologists have found skeletal remains under floors, in walls, next to walls, in or near ovens and hearths, and under thresholds. With altars and hearths in their homes dedicated to ancestors, the ancient Greeks and Romans continued this practice, at least in spirit; and Christians in Europe, for the better part of a thousand years (and sometimes still), modified the practice by burying the dead beneath the floors of their churches and by venerating the relics of saints.[40] Harrison again: "It is as if we the living can stand only because the dead underlie the ground on which we build our homes, worlds, commonwealths."[41]

The morgue at Rema Hospital was Maggy's way of embodying the insight of these ancient practices. During the war, she came to understand that once the dead are simply dead, everything human begins to withdraw. "Some truths are glimpsed only in the dark," Harrison says. "That is why in moments of extreme need one must turn to those who can see through the gloom. The primary reason the dead have an afterlife in so many cultures is because it falls to them to come to the rescue and provide counsel when the debilitating darkness falls."[42] The morgue at Rema Hospital was Maggy's way of letting the dead counsel the living.

There is a real if metaphorical sense that the unkempt cemetery near the compound of the bishop underlies everything Maggy created after the traumatic events of October 1993. She buried the dead there and then paid tribute to them with a memorial. "Here rest the 72 victims of 24 October 1993. Dear parents, dear friends, rest in peace."[43] Maggy built Maison Shalom on those foundations as a testament to the fact that, in the words of Michael Barnett, "the dead deserve not only cemeteries but also moral institutions."[44] That, it seems, is the cost of their counsel.

When she still lived in Ruyigi, Maggy made regular visits to the grave of the seventy-two and always took visitors there as well. "Not to relive the trauma," she says, "but so that I might see the future more clearly." Despite any foresight Maggy might have gained, however, the future came as a surprise. On May 14, 2015, the president of Burundi sent men to kill her.

PART TWO

Exile

Build houses and live in them; plant gardens and eat what they produce. Seek the welfare of the city where I have sent you into exile, and pray to the Lord on its behalf, for in its welfare you will find your welfare. For surely I know the plans I have for you, says the Lord, plans for your welfare and not for harm, to give you a future with hope.

—Jeremiah 29:5, 7, 11

The attempt on Maggy's life in 2015 was not the first. That came early in the war when a rebel child soldier stopped her at a checkpoint, ordered her out of the car, and told her to kneel. Her response was to say, "I only kneel for God, but I will kneel down to pray, if you kneel down with me." Then she noticed that he was wearing a rosary around his neck. "Why do you carry a gun and a rosary? You know, the two don't go well together. If you give back the gun and come with me, I will give you something better to do." The boy ran into the bush. The next day, he showed up at Maison Shalom, without the gun. Intensely loyal to Maggy, he's been with Maison Shalom ever since.

Another attempt on Maggy's life occurred on December 31, 2007, when the governor of Ruyigi Province sent someone to kill her. The gunman, however, mistook the car of a French NGO for Maggy's vehicle and killed a French aid worker. Realizing his mistake, he planted the murder weapon at the house of a woman who worked for Maggy, who was then accused of ordering the killing.

At a hearing on the incident, the local government had packed the courtroom with people yelling at Maggy, "You are a criminal. You are a killer." The scene was reminiscent of the tribunal that took place in 1995, when Maggy testified about the massacre of October 1993. Some of the killers, including members of her own family, were in the courtroom. Maggy addressed them: "Come, stand up. I have seen you. You have killed in front of me."

A Tutsi accusing other Tutsi, let alone relatives, of murdering Hutu was an unforgivable breach of ethnic protocol. Inside the courtroom, the scene was tense. Outside, a Tutsi mob had formed. Carrying stones and bamboo sticks, they yelled insults and threats. When Maggy finished testifying, a friend whose house was nearby whisked her away to safety. "They threw stones at me, they called me a murderer. I saw people rejoicing and celebrating believing that I was going to exile myself, but I refused to let myself be impressed." Aside from a few token arrests, nothing came of Maggy's testimony.

In 2007, circumstances were different. The accusation against her was clearly absurd, and the court dismissed the case. But for Maggy the trumped-up charge and courtroom chants that echoed those from 1995 occasioned deep despair. It's in that context that she told me the story. I had asked, "Have you had moments of despair similar to the moment in the chapel in 1993 before you realized your children were alive?" In reply, she told me of the attempt on her life, the false accusation, and the courtroom drama. Then she said, "I bought a ticket to leave Burundi. I didn't even tell my brother or my children. I said, 'This is not a country.'"

At the airport, the young woman who took Maggy's ticket recognized her. "Maggy, you are very sad, no smile. What happened? Did you lose a member of your family? Are you going to a funeral?" The words of concern brought Maggy up short. "This lady, she continued to believe in me. What she said came from the heart. I thought, 'These questions come from God.'"

The comment made me think of a biblical story about the prophet Balaam, in the Book of Numbers. He was traveling on an errand against clear instructions from God when "an angel of the Lord took his stand in the road as his adversary" (Numbers 22:22). I asked Maggy, "So was that actually God standing in your way? Like the angel on the path of the prophet Balaam?" She replied, "Yes. And that's why I left the airport to return to the *champ de bataille* . . . the field of battle."

I asked Maggy about occasions of despair one other time. "One thing we haven't talked about is the silence of God, if that was ever a reality in your dark moments, or in your—the harder moments . . ." I hadn't finished asking the question when Maggy answered. "Even now. Even now, I try to understand why we suffered during twelve years of war. Why now God has given us a criminal president. I don't understand why God keeps abandoning us. We're tired. The Burundian people are tired."

Maggy went on to explain that when she feels abandoned, she works, and that in this case that meant trying to meet with Burundi's president. "I have pity on him," she said. "How can he keep all that . . ." She paused, searching for words, and then, "How can a person be a criminal and stay in the darkness? Last week I went to the archbishop and said, 'We can go in a group to meet the president, only to say we want to understand. We want to advise you. We want to tell you that we love you.' And the archbishop said, 'Me, return to this president? No.' I said, 'If you can't go, who can?' He said, 'You—you can go.'" Maggy laughed at the thought and then said, "This is God's silence." She laughed because she had met with the president ten months earlier, to no effect.

~

The leader of a Hutu rebel group during the civil war, Pierre Nkurunziza had been elected Burundi's president in 2005 by both houses of a newly formed parliament and then reelected by the people in 2010. That was the process laid out a decade earlier in the Arusha Accords, a ninety-three-page blueprint for putting the country back together after a civil war that was tearing it apart.[1] The Accords called for a three-year transitional government that would follow a series of steps to reconstitute Burundi as a democracy: first the creation of a new parliament (a National Assembly and a Senate) via local elections; followed by the parliamentary drafting of a new constitution approved by the people in a referendum; then the election of a president, not, at first, via a national election but by a two-thirds majority of parliament voting in a joint session.

All that came to pass, in five years not three, when Burundi's parliament took the last step and elected Nkurunziza as president in August 2005. Ironically, it was that step in putting Burundi back together again that led to its eventual undoing, because Nkurunziza used that opening check on undue presidential power to manipulate his way into an unconstitutional third term. That was the topic of discussion when Maggy met with the archbishop in January 2015 and suggested that they go together to meet with Nkurunziza, who had spent the previous year showing clear signs that he had become, in Maggy's words, "a criminal president."

Even in 2010, when he was elected by the people not by parliament, there were signs that Nkurunziza was off course. Leading into the elections, he had arrested and imprisoned leaders of the opposition and organized militias to attack and intimidate their supporters. The arrests and violence led several opposition parties to boycott the election on grounds that it would not be free and fair.[2] In 2014, however, with 2015 elections looming, Nkurunziza amplified his attempts to stay in power, first by proposing constitutional amendments and then by marshaling a dubious interpretation of the constitution.

On March 21, a vote in the National Assembly fell one vote short of passing Nkurunziza's proposed amendments with the required four-fifths majority.[3] The immediate response of the CNDD-FDD, the ruling political party, was to say that Nkurunziza was eligible to run in 2015 even without an amended constitution.[4] They argued he was eligible for a third term because the parliament and not the people had elected him to his first term in 2005. The people had elected him only once, in 2010. The chair of the CNDD-FDD had tested that argument in 2013, in an address to a provincial party congress, laying groundwork for a backup plan to constitutional amendments.[5] When those amendments failed to pass the National Assembly, Nkurunziza and the CNDD-FDD threw everything they had into their "elected-only-once" argument.

~

On March 12, nine days before the National Assembly failed to pass Nkurunziza's proposed constitutional amendments, Maggy met with him privately. She remembers the date because it was the first week of Lent and the Old Testament reading for the day was Jonah 3:1–10:

> The word of the Lord came to Jonah a second time, saying, "Get up, go to Nineveh, that great city, and proclaim to it the message that I tell you." So Jonah set out and went to Nineveh, according to the word of the Lord. And he cried out, "Forty days more, and Nineveh shall be overthrown!" When the news reached the king of Nineveh, he rose from his throne, removed his robe, covered himself with sackcloth, and sat in ashes. Then he had a proclamation made in Nineveh: "All shall turn from their evil ways and from

the violence that is in their hands. Who knows? God may relent and change his mind; he may turn from his fierce anger, so that we do not perish."

Maggy starts each day by reading the biblical passages in the lectionary. Then she says the same prayer: "Lord, make your wonders shine, and let me not be an obstacle." When she read the passage from Jonah that morning in March 2014, she cried. "I will show you where my tears stained the page." She shed tears because later in the day she was scheduled to meet with Nkurunziza. A Catholic who had taken a fundamentalist turn, he believed that God had called him to be president. When she read the words from Jonah, Maggy knew she was being called to tell Nkurunziza that God might have other plans.

Confrontational meetings with government officials were not unusual for Maggy. "When we are in political meetings and I see a minister joking, taking all these things lightly, I stand up and say, 'Stop. You don't know what your brothers, your sisters, your parents have suffered. Don't lead us again to see mothers burned in their houses, or the hands of our friends in the mouths of dogs on the street." Confrontations like this had become Maggy's *modus operandi*, but she had yet to speak this way in a one-on-one meeting with the president of the country. She had met Nkurunziza once before, in 2008; but on that occasion, he was honoring the work of Maison Shalom and praising Maggy publicly as Mother of the Nation.

When I inquired how the president responded when Maggy delivered Jonah's message, she said, "I was not talking to a human being. I could see it in his eyes. You can argue with God. You cannot argue with evil. Its purpose is to confuse." Her reply reminded me of Canadian general Roméo Dallaire's experiences overseeing the UN peacekeeping mission during the Rwandan genocide. The role required that he meet with the government officials orchestrating the genocide. Asked how he could still believe in God after what he had experienced in Rwanda, he said, "I know there is a God because in Rwanda I shook hands with the devil. I have seen him, I have smelled him, and I have touched him. I know the devil exists, and therefore I know there is a God."[6]

After she met with Nkurunziza, Maggy never spoke with him again in person; but she did address him from a distance, in a speech at a conference in Paris in August 2015, in which she cast herself not as Jonah but as Joan of Arc, the young woman who, inspired by divine visions, led French troops into battle and turned the tide of the Hundred Years' War in favor of the French against the English. When the English captured Joan of Arc and she refused to recant her claim that God was the source of her role in French victories, the English convicted her of heresy.

"They burned her at the stake," Maggy reminds me. "This is the picture I conveyed to the president when I was in Paris. I said, 'Nkurunziza! If you want war again, then I will become Joan of Arc. Maggy will be the first woman to oppose you, and you can burn me, but I will not let you make war again. No, no, no—I will go in front with others to say, Stop. We can't accept that you are again leading us into darkness.'"

~

Maggy met privately with Nkurunziza in March 2014. She railed against him publicly from Paris in August 2015. The seventeen months in between were a tipping point for the country—and for Maggy. First came the failed constitutional amendments, followed by the public airing of the "elected-only-once" argument. Then in May 2014, Bujumbura police arrested Pierre Mbonimpa, a well-known human rights activist and president of the Burundian Association for the Protection of Human Rights and Detained Persons. Police interrogated

Mbonimpa about his criticism of Burundi's security services while appearing on a radio talk show. Among other things, he had denounced the distribution of weapons to the *Imbonerakure*, the youth wing of the ruling party.[7] At the time, they numbered about a thousand and had been implicated in beatings, acts of extortion, and intimidation of the CNDD-FDD's political opponents.[8]

Maggy's response to Mbonimpa's arrest was to help organize Green Tuesdays, weekly marches through the streets of Bujumbura with participants dressed in green, the color of prison uniforms. Her stamp on the marches was readily apparent: people carried candles while singing the Prayer of St. Francis. The marches continued even after Mbonimpa's provisional release at the end of September. Meanwhile, the CNDD-FDD continued to press Nkurunziza's case for a third term. In November, however, most former generals in the FDD—the armed wing of the CNDD during the war and thus colleagues of Nkurunziza—spoke out against his push to stay in power.[9]

As 2014 came to a close, Burundi seemed to be on the precipice of another war, or at least escalating violence, which is what led Maggy to propose to the archbishop in the opening weeks of 2015 that they try to meet with Nkurunziza. The idea didn't gain traction, but it might not have mattered. On January 20, the terms of engagement changed. That's the day Bujumbura police arrested Bob Rugurika, director of Radio Publique Africaine, "the voice of the people." In a country where radio is the dominant medium, RPA was Burundi's most popular station. Not coincidentally, it was also the station that had aired the program that led to Pierre Mbonimpa's arrest eight months earlier.

Bob Rugurika and Maggy were friends, and he called Maggy shortly after his arrest. Maggy went to meet him. "I will show you when I was with him in prison," she says. "I keep the photo because it's so profound for me." Maggy scrolls through her phone and finds the picture. It shows Maggy and Bob standing side by side in the office of the prison warden, with Bob still in his street clothes. Between them is a large bouquet of fresh flowers. "Imagine," Maggy says, "I went with flowers." The photograph is profound for Maggy because Bob had called her from prison to give her an assignment: she needed to start speaking out not only for children but for the country against a repressive government. Maggy was scared and uncertain about the role.

On February 19, the government released Bob, in what may have been a miscalculation. Thousands of people flocked to the streets to greet him. "It was a powerful message to the government," Bob recalled, "to show them that the population is tired of injustices and human rights violations, especially ones which implicate the government. I must say that my release scared the government. The government then felt defeated and has since changed the methods of prosecution."[10]

Nkurunziza's new methods for combating opposition and securing his power varied. In part, he employed the political process. On April 25, the CNDD-FDD officially nominated him for a third term. At the same time, he went after public support for the opposition. The day after the announcement of his candidacy, the government banned Bob's radio station and two other popular radio programs from live reporting.

The announcement of Nkurunziza's candidacy combined with growing repression led to massive protests in the streets of Bujumbura on April 26. Maggy had just returned to the city after being in Ruyigi for the inauguration of her latest invention: the Centre de Rééducation pour Mineurs au Burundi, the capstone to a project she had started six years earlier with Maria Teresa, grand duchess of Luxembourg, whom Maggy refers to simply as "the queen." Working with the ministry of justice, UNICEF, and others, Maria Teresa and Maggy had pushed for a facility to house minors convicted of crimes, to separate them from the adult prison population. Maria Teresa was not with

Maggy for the inauguration of the new center, but when men came to kill Maggy two weeks later, she would become a key figure in Maggy's story.

The inauguration of the new facility in Ruyigi took place on April 24. Maggy left immediately after the ceremony for Bujumbura, aware of the growing tensions in the city, which erupted into massive protests two days later. Until then, Maggy had remained tentative about Bob Rugurika's plea that she speak out for the country. Her tipping point came on the first day of the protests, when police killed Jean Népomuscène Komezamahoro, a sixteen-year-old bystander. Witnesses to his death said that he was running away from the protests when he stumbled on some stones and fell. He tried to explain to the police that he was not a demonstrator but simply a kid trying to get out of the way, but the police didn't back off. When an officer shot him in the head, Népo was on his knees, begging for his life.[11]

~

I've said earlier in several places that Maggy's story resists chronology, and I've guessed at the reasons: traumatic memory, or a panoptic or panoramic vision that allows her to see everything at once. I could add that she has given thousands of interviews and in the process honed a sense of what fits the moment and what doesn't, which means that interlocutors like me are often getting only a flash of color in the kaleidoscope of a life. Over the years, I've learned in my conversations with Maggy that often the most telling thing about her is not the story she tells, or where it fits in a chronological sequence, but what prompts her to tell it.

I heard about Népo's death from Maggy in a surprising way. We weren't talking about the crises in Burundi or about the attempt on her life in 2015. Rather, I was pressing her for details about the years before the Carmelite monastery, the years when she was so angry. I was confirming various stories I had heard. Had a priest really had to intervene when she saw a man at Mass wearing Cyprian's clothes? Had she really attacked a soldier when he called her children snakes?

"Yes," she said. "Of course, I never actually hit anyone. It was only on the inside. I killed them in my heart. But this was before I prayed and reconciled with myself and learned how to forgive." Maggy paused and then punctuated the silence: "BUT . . . in 2015 I had the same reaction. What I saw again in 2015, imagine, I was more angry than before. You can see it when I was on TV. Here, I'll show you a photo."

Maggy reached for her cell phone and began scrolling through her photographs, something that was now common when we talked. She uses the images on her phone as a visual archive of her life and work, sometimes pulling up photographs, other times videos she has stored away or grabbed from YouTube. The photograph she landed on showed her on the street in Bujumbura, outside the president's office. "After they killed Népo, I joined the protests. The police cleared the streets, but I refused to leave. 'You will never kill my children. I prefer to die.'" Unsure what to do, the police left Maggy alone on the street in front of the president's office, screaming about injustice.

The photographer caught Maggy, in the middle of a word, her mouth open, her face contorted in anger, both arms outstretched, in a pose that was almost cruciform, except that her arms pitched up and away from her body, as if she were grabbing hold of the world and shaking it awake from its slumber.

When I asked Maggy why she was so angry, she explained that the people responsible for killing Népo were the rebels who had become the government. "During the war, they also suffered so much, and I saved them. I sacrificed for them. I risked my life for them. I hid their children to save them from the Tutsi army. Now they were killing children, and I felt betrayed." I realized as Maggy told me the story that once again she was describing her visceral reaction to betrayal, just as she had when telling me of the massacre in Butezi.

~

On May 4, barely a week after protests started, and with Bujumbura in disarray, the Constitutional Court, under clear political pressure, ruled that Nkurunziza was eligible to run for another term. They had accepted the argument that his first term didn't count because he was elected by the National Assembly as part of forming a new government, and not by the people. The slightly delayed response from the opposition was an attempted coup.

On May 13, facing the prospect of five more years with Nkurunziza as president, a faction of the Burundian army tried but failed to unseat him. Early the next day, Nkurunziza's supporters attacked the headquarters of Radio Publique Africaine in Bujumbura and left the building in flames. The same day, Maggy was in her car traveling across Bujumbura to visit her brother. As her driver picked his way through Bujumbura traffic, Maggy received a text message: "We have been sent to kill you. We know where you are going. Don't go there." Maggy showed the text to her driver. "We must go to the Belgian ambassador." Her driver changed course, and Maggy called the grand duchess of Luxembourg.

Maggy and Maria Teresa had met in 2009 when the duchess visited Maison Shalom and Maggy introduced her to a crisis in Burundi's prisons: they were filling up with children. Prison visits had been part of Maggy's life since she was young. "Every Sunday after Mass, we celebrated a 'second Mass' in prison. We brought food to the prisoners, who had nothing to eat. It was part of my education from my mom." When Maria Teresa reached out to plan a visit to Maison Shalom, Maggy saw an opportunity. She would seek permission from Burundi's minister of justice to take the duchess to the prisons.

The Belgian ambassador (who also serves as the ambassador for Luxembourg) told Maggy she was crazy: "Nobody will accept taking the duchess into Burundian prisons. It's very dangerous. They can kill you." Maggy responded, "No. It's not dangerous. Because when I enter a prison and the prisoners see me, they know that I love them, because I am the only woman who comes each week and brings them things. Then I said to the ambassador, 'I will protect the queen. Nobody will hurt her. We are just two crazy women, and we will go.'"

After visiting Burundi's prisons with Maggy, the duchess made freeing minors who had committed petty crimes—or no crimes at all—one of her causes. Commenting later she said, "No one expected the wife of a royal and a head of state to go into a Burundi prison. But I am a Latin, with a Latin temperament. I always say and do what I believe. And my causes have never been at all usual."[12] This commitment to unusual causes is perhaps what led the grand duchess, a Cuban by birth who married into European royalty, to befriend Maggy.

Of her relationship with Maria Teresa, Maggy might say what she said when I asked her if either *The Sound of Music* or *Gone with the Wind* had been her inspiration for turning the bishop's curtains into children's clothes. She said she had never even heard of these stories. When I described the scene from *The Sound of Music* in which Maria makes clothes for the seven Von Trapp children after Captain von Trapp, their stern father, refuses her request for material, Maggy laughed and said, "Strong women always have the same dreams."

Maggy's response to the text message from the men sent to kill her was to call Maria Teresa. "Immediately, I phoned the queen. I said, 'I am in danger' and asked her to call the ambassador of Belgium to see if I could go to him. I knew I was asking something political, that I couldn't seek refuge without permission, which would have to come from Belgium's minister of foreign affairs. Belgium and Luxembourg have close ties, and I knew the queen could help."

The Belgian ambassador was Marc Gedopt. He was in his fourth year in the role and knew Maggy well. When Maggy tells the story, she jumps straight to the outcome of her call to the queen, so it's not clear if her driver headed straight for the embassy or for the ambassador's residence or if he simply drove around awaiting a call back from Maria Teresa. Whatever happened in those tense minutes, the outcome was arrival at the ambassador's residence. He had received permission to take her into his home, not the embassy.

Who knows how the killers explained their failure, but the result was a "manhunt" for Maggy. At first, the government thought she might have sought refuge in the apostolic nunciature, the Vatican's diplomatic mission. Then they switched their suspicions to the Belgian embassy. Meanwhile, Maggy was hiding in the ambassador's residence. She was there for a month.

"I was in a small room, with its own bathroom. It was the meditation room for the ambassador's wife. At first, she was not there. The ambassador would bring me coffee in the morning, and food. He was worried I would be depressed. I was always alone, until his wife came back. Then we would visit. One day she came when I was putting on my perfume and makeup. She was surprised because I couldn't leave the small room. I said to her, 'Why must I die before my death? I must celebrate life.'"

Maggy's celebration led to her discovery. She has a habit of singing, and men from one of Nkurunziza's militias heard singing every morning when they were in a nearby garden. They reported it. "She is there," they said. "We hear singing, but we never see anybody." Maggy also made the mistake of using her cell phone, which allowed the government to confirm that she was hiding in the ambassador's residence. Burundi's government demanded that Belgium turn over Maggy. When the ambassador declined, they threatened to send men to his house to take her by force.

The ambassador called a meeting with Maggy and his staff and asked Maggy what she wanted to do. That's when she hatched an elaborate plan for escape. "We will arrange tickets for a commercial flight to Brussels," she said, "and I will go through customs dressed as a prostitute. I know how stupid they are." The ambassador protested, "No, they will kill you in front of me."

It was not a misplaced fear. Three weeks earlier, while Maggy was hiding in the ambassador's residence, Zedi Feruzi, a vocal critic of Nkurunziza, had been shot while in his car on the way home from work. And in the months after Maggy's escape, three other prominent critics of Nkurunziza were murdered in Bujumbura and a fourth was seriously injured: Pierre Claver Mbonimpa, whose arrest had been the inspiration for Green Tuesdays, was shot on August 3. He survived, but later several members of his family were killed.[13]

Maggy's response to the ambassador was to say, "They won't kill me. You'll see." Then she convinced him to make the arrangements, which included working with Brussels Airlines to make sure her name did not appear on the manifest. After that, everything rested on Maggy.

On June 17, they headed from the ambassador's house to the airport with Maggy dressed like a prostitute—sunglasses, a blond wig, long nails, huge earrings, and lots of makeup. Accompanying the ambassador and other dignitaries, she flaunted her way through the small airport and went straight to a VIP room to await boarding and avoid normal check-in procedures. Once when she told me the story, she acted out her role, rising from where we sat in the hotel lobby and showing me how she sashayed alongside the ambassador, swinging her hips, tossing her hair, bumping into people and saying, "Hi.

Hi. Sorry, sorry, sorry." Laughing as she reenacted the scene, she described the ambassador. "He was shaking."

Once time for boarding came, Maggy's escape plan included the use of two passports. That would have been easy in years past because she used to carry both a regular passport and a Burundian diplomatic passport, but she had turned in the latter to the government in 2014. Her substitute in this case was an old passport and a new one. Back in April, she had realized that her passport was almost out of pages, so she went to immigration to get a new one and convinced the person in immigration to let her keep her old passport instead of destroying it. Explaining the kind of planning that comes from years of insecurity, she says, "It was corruption, but it was during the protests."

At the airport, still playing the part of the prostitute and surrounded by an entourage of diplomats, Maggy handed the old passport to the customs officer and headed for the tarmac without waiting for the officer to return her passport. The ruse bought her just enough time. "They tried to follow me. But it was too late because the plan was prepared." Brussels Airlines is Belgium's national airline, and the crew was ready for a quick departure.

When Maggy made it to her seat on the plane she found that she was seated near Burundi's minister of justice. He changed seats. After that, the long flight to Brussels was uneventful. By the time the plane arrived, Burundi had done whatever you do in the global systems of passport control to revoke her new passport. It turned out that she could have left that one behind too. In the matter of a few hours, Maggy had become both a fugitive and a refugee.

～

In Belgium, the prime minister had prepared immigration for Maggy's arrival, and the grand duchess had arranged a car to bring her to Luxembourg City, the capital of Luxembourg, a drive of three hours or so. "Two days later," Maggy says, "I was at the table with the king and queen, and my brother and two nieces, and my sister-in-law. And I said, 'My place is not in the palace. I will go now. I am ready to go to fight among my people. I will go to Mahama.'" Mahama was the location of a refugee camp that UNHCR had set up in Rwanda in April 2015—almost literally overnight, as tens of thousands of people fled Burundi in the turmoil of Nkurunziza's increasingly violent and oppressive attempt to stay in power. By the time of Maggy's escape in mid-June, the camp was home to nearly thirty thousand Burundians.

Maria Teresa responded, "But, Maggy, Rwanda is near Burundi. They will kill you. And you have nothing." Maggy replied, "I have you, and you are the queen. If I stay here, you will take care of me. Won't you also come to take care of me when I am among my people?" The duchess laughed. "Yes, this is Maggy." Then she helped Maggy make plans for traveling to Rwanda. "She was thinking," Maggy says, "that of course I would come back to live. I was thinking that Rwanda would let me live there, not in Kigali, but in Mahama. But the government would not let me live in the camp."

When Maggy first recounted the details of her escape from Burundi, I was curious about her decision to flee. After all, once before she had decided to leave after a failed attempt on her life but turned back at the airport, convinced that God wanted her to rejoin the *champ de bataille*. "When you were still in Bujumbura and you knew they wanted to kill you, did you think you should stay?"

"At first I refused to flee," she said. "The ambassadors from the European Union and the African Union and others said, 'You must go. You must flee, Maggy. We don't want them to kill you in this country. Please go.' I said, 'How can a mother flee and leave her children? Burundi is suffering. I can't go.

Yes, they might kill me, but I will be here among my children. I don't want to leave.' They said, 'We'll give you time.'"

During the month she was in hiding, Maggy sought advice about what to do, not least from her children—a large group without clear boundaries. It includes her formally adopted children plus Lydia and Lysette, but also many others drawn from the tens of thousands Maison Shalom took in over more than two decades, as well as Burundians from the diaspora whom she sees as sons and daughters.

The advice that stuck came from Lydia, who had become part of the diaspora and lived in Canada. "I called her and said, 'Lydia, tell me what I must do. If I stay here, they will kill me. But if I flee, I will die outside Burundi without my children. Without my mother Burundi.' Lydia laughed. 'Stop being stupid. That's what you say. Now I'm saying it to you. Stop being stupid. You can't save your people if you die. Be humble and leave. Be like Joseph, who saved Israel while in Egypt.'" That's the counsel that led to Maggy's decision to flee. "I thought of Joseph, and I prayed. 'Be humble.' Then I let the ambassador know I would go."

Reflecting on the decision when we met in Rwanda just over a year after her escape, Maggy said, "Now I realize that everyone who wanted me to flee was right." It was July 2016, and she was settling into life as a refugee after attaining that status officially from Luxembourg. It had been a little over a year since her escape. By then, UNHCR had recorded the flight of 275,682 Burundians from Burundi into neighboring countries. More than 30,000 Burundian refugees were congregating in Kigali; more than 50,000 were crammed into the tents of Mahama refugee camp sixty miles to the east. Altogether, more than 160,000 Burundian refugees were living in Rwanda at the time, among them 2,139 unaccompanied children, with which Maggy was all too familiar.[14]

Maggy was a refugee among refugees, with a growing sense

that somehow it was meant to be. "They need me," she said, adding, "The way of God is always surprising. I am now grateful and humble. Like Mary, when the angel came, I am the servant. My response—my answer to God. 'Oh God, let your will be done.' I am full of peace and gratitude. I don't understand. No. I don't understand. In Burundi, they continue to kill my children, my cousins, but God is God, and he cannot abandon his people. If I obey, I know there will be so many miraculous things."

~

While Maggy was settling into Kigali in the months following her escape, Maison Shalom in Burundi, with a full-time staff of 270, was still functioning in her absence under the able leadership of Richard Nijimbere. Like most of the staff, he was a former child of Maison Shalom, having come to Maggy as an orphan back in 1997. His Hutu parents were killed on October 24, 1993, the same day Maggy survived the attack in the bishop's compound. Richard was thirteen when the Tutsi killers set the roof of his boyhood home on fire and then shot his family members as they fled the house to escape the flames.

After watching through a window as the killers murdered his parents, Richard stayed in the house and hid under a table. When the roof caved in and the table burst into flames, he stayed beneath it as long as he could. Finally, deciding it was better to die from bullets than flames, he ran from the building expecting to be shot, but by then the killers had gone. Badly burned, he would have died were it not for an uncle who refused to give up on him. With his uncle's help, he made it to a refugee camp in Tanzania, where he stayed for four months before returning to Burundi to live with his grandparents.

In July 1997, his grandparents were killed. With no family left, he made his way to Ruyigi and showed up at Maison Shalom. He was seventeen years old. In 2003, Maggy sent

Richard to Russia for an education because it was affordable, especially if you opted for classes in Russian instead of English. Richard lived in Russia for six years: two years to learn the language and four to earn a degree in economics and finance. In 2009, he returned to Burundi and took over the management of Maison Shalom's field operations.[15] Many of the staff of Maison Shalom in Burundi had stories like Richard's.

"We went on working after Maggy left," Richard told me. "We had some challenges, of course, because of what was happening in the country, but we continued with our everyday activities." Back in April and May 2015, he explained, rumors that Maggy was funding some of the men who were challenging Nkurunziza had fed the idea that she was part of the political opposition and the attempted coup. After Maggy fled, Richard said, "We began to hear rumors that this assumption was being applied to Maison Shalom as well and that the government was not just angry with Maggy. We saw the first clear sign on November 4." That's when the government seized all of Maison Shalom's financial assets—roughly $3.5 million.

At the time, eighty-five of Rema Hospital's 120 beds were occupied with inpatients who were not ready for discharge, and suddenly no funds were available for medicine, or for salaries past November 15. Richard spent the next six days negotiating with the government via email and phone, trying to find a solution, but he was either ignored or threatened. Meanwhile, doctors and nurses volunteered to work for free until they could safely discharge the last of the patients.

Twice, government officials agreed to meet Richard in person, but each time they changed the location at the last minute. The second time, they moved the location to a town that made Richard suspicious. Bad things had happened there back in 1993 and again in 1997. The meeting there was scheduled for November 10. That morning, Richard told his staff he was going to meet with the government and instead drove north across the border into Rwanda, where he joined Maggy.

Thirteen days later, the government issued decree 530/1597, which suspended the activities of ten non-governmental organizations in Burundi, among them Maison Shalom.[16] Effectively, Maison Shalom had become an enemy of the state. In the months that followed, other staff joined Richard and Maggy in exile in Rwanda, and Maison Shalom was on its way to becoming a Rwandan NGO run by Burundian refugees for Burundian refugees and for anyone else in the region being forced to flee their home country.

~

Following her escape, Maggy recognized that she was being pressed into something new, but she was unsure of what it might be. In the April protests, she had taken Bob Rugurika's plea to heart and spoken out for her country—motivated in no small measure by the death of Népo. Now she was a refugee in exile. She had left Burundi with nothing. She was sleeping on a mattress in a house with other refugees, some of whom had sewn the clothes she was wearing. She had some sense that she had become untethered from what she had been doing since 1993, but she was uneasy. "At first, I was shy and said, 'No, I can't. I don't want to do new things. I will go to church and pray alone, and I will help orphans and send young people to school.'"

It's not surprising that Maggy wanted to go back to helping orphans. "There is a difference," she notes, "between speaking out for children and speaking out for a country." For Maggy, that difference showed up in a text message from men sent to kill her, in a month of hiding, and in her flight into exile. It appeared again on October 12, four months after her escape, when Burundi's attorney general issued international arrest warrants for Maggy and eleven other Burundians living in exile. All were charged with "illegal possession of firearms, participation in an insurrectional movement, intentional grievous assault and battery, intentional destruction, murder and breach of national security."[17]

In those first months of exile, Maggy started looking for a sign, for some indication that God might have something new in mind for her. He had preserved her life in 1993, and in the bishop's chapel she had recognized that her vocation was to create a new generation in Burundi, one that left behind the myth of Tutsi and Hutu ethnicity. He had stopped her at the airport in 2007, when she had decided to give up on her country, and gently pushed her back into the Burundian field of battle. Now he had saved her life again, but with the result that she was living in exile. What was the plan? Maggy received a clue on April 24, 2016, when she became the inaugural laureate of the Aurora Prize for Awakening Humanity.

The Aurora Prize is a unique award, and Maggy was uniquely fit to be the first recipient. The prize is named after Aurora Mardiganian. At thirteen, Aurora witnessed the murder of her family during the Armenian genocide and was then sold into slavery. Eventually, she escaped to the United States. In 1919, she starred as herself in the silent film *Ravished Armenia*, an attempt to alert the world to the systematic killing of nearly a million Armenians in 1915 (and more in the years that followed). A poster for the film described its content: "The tremendous motion picture spectacle of the great massacres, through which runs the tender, heart-gripping story of Aurora Mardiganian, the Christian girl who survived. A vivid, authentic portrayal of the greatest tragedy the world has ever witnessed."[18]

The Armenian genocide holds a prominent place in the history of humanity. In 1919, "the greatest tragedy the world has ever witnessed" was what Raphael Lemkin would later call a "crime without a name." Lemkin is justly renowned for coining the term *genocide* and, even more, for spending years convincing the world to make genocide a crime in international law. His efforts began in 1921 when he read a news story about the assassination of Mehmed Talaat, the Turkish interior minister who had orchestrated the mass killing of Armenians. Soghomon Tehlirian, an Armenian survivor, shot Talaat on the street in Berlin and was being tried for murder. Talaat, on the other hand, had never been charged with a crime. Lemkin was confused. "It is a crime for Tehlirian to kill a man, but it is not a crime for his oppressor to kill more than a million men? That is most inconsistent."[19]

The United Nations ratified the Convention on the Prevention and Punishment of the Crime of Genocide in 1948, but even now the Turkish government does not acknowledge the mass murder of Armenians as genocide, and the events themselves, the ones dramatized in *Ravished Armenia*, are largely forgotten. The Aurora Prize was created in 2015, the hundredth anniversary of the genocide, "on behalf of the survivors . . . and in gratitude to their saviors." The goal, built into the name of the prize, was to awaken humanity from the trance that enables genocide and other horrific acts of violence that continue to plague the world—often on a massive scale. The method was "to recognize modern day heroes and the exceptional impact their actions have made on preserving human life and advancing humanitarian causes in the face of adversity."[20]

With all that in play in the background, a selection committee co-chaired by Elie Wiesel—Holocaust survivor and Nobel Peace Prize laureate—chose Maggy as the inaugural recipient of the prize, which included a $1 million award.[21] Maggy had received a $1 million award once before—the Opus Prize in 2008, a faith-based award for social entrepreneurship that recognizes remarkable people who "combine the spirit of innovation with amazing faith to inspire long-term, local solutions to address poverty and injustice."[22] But the Aurora Prize was different, and the significance and honor were not lost on Maggy. It was more than praise for her innovative solutions to poverty and injustice in Burundi. The award acknowledged Maggy as an advocate for humanity in the face of the inhuman.

The award ceremony was held in Yerevan, Armenia. George Clooney, co-chair of the selection committee, welcomed Maggy to the stage. The audience had just watched a short film highlighting Maggy's work in Burundi. The film ended with Maggy speaking of the victory of love over hatred. She opened her brief acceptance speech by saying, "Yes, it is the victory of love over hatred, despite what I felt this morning visiting your memorial."

Maggy told me about the experience of receiving the award when we were together in Rwanda in July 2016. Only three months had passed since her trip to Armenia. She asked, "Did you see the ceremony?" I told her I had, having found it on the web. "Then you saw me crying when George Clooney greeted me after announcing my name?" That I had missed, but I did hear the quaver in her voice when she spoke of the victory of love over hatred; and when the camera zoomed in, I could see that her eyes had welled with tears.

I've since gone back to watch the moment Clooney announces Maggy as "the first, the very first recipient of the Aurora Prize for Awakening Humanity." She is standing on stage with members of the selection committee and three other finalists. Clooney is at a microphone a few feet in front of the group. He opens an envelope, reads Maggy's name, and turns toward her. Smiling, Maggy dances forward a few steps to meet him. Clooney embraces her, kissing each cheek, and then steps back to say something. For the briefest moment before it cuts away, the camera catches Maggy dropping her head and raising her hand to wipe away a tear.

"I cried because I was afraid," Maggy said. "All the young people, even my friends in Europe, they were saying, 'Maggy, you must do something.' The queen said, 'Maggy, you cannot let your people die.' I asked God for a sign. I said, 'I am a refugee, a beggar. What am I supposed to do?' Then to win this award—a humanitarian award to awaken humanity, and for me to be the first . . ." She didn't finish her sentence.

It's tempting at this point in Maggy's story to say that she now knew what she was supposed to do. Cut off from Burundi and a life defined by advocacy for children, she would become a citizen of the world, an advocate for humanity, a global messenger of love and peace. It's tempting to tell the story that way because sometimes that's how Maggy tells it. The Aurora Prize was a turning point, the sign she needed, "a humanitarian award to awaken humanity, and for me to be the first . . ."

In 2016, however, a lot was going on in that unfinished sentence. You could hear it at the end of her Aurora Prize acceptance speech: "Thank you. Thank you, to you Armenians for giving me courage and giving me strength to think I can go back, and one day I will go back to my country and sing our own national anthem."[23] Adopted at independence in 1962, a few lines of Burundi's national anthem reveal what was most on Maggy's mind when she accepted the Aurora Prize:

> Our Burundi, gentle country / take your place in the concert of nations. / Wounded and bruised, you have remained master of yourself. / When the hour came, you arose / lifting yourself proudly into the ranks of free peoples. / Receive, then, the congratulations of the nations / and the homage of your sons and daughters. / May your name ring out through the universe. / May your name ring out through the universe. / Our Burundi, sacred heritage from our forefathers / worthy of our tenderest love / we vow to your noble service our hands and hearts and lives.[24]

The Aurora Prize was a transition in the arc of Maggy's life; and in the years since, she has increasingly devoted herself to "humanizing humanity," as she puts it. But the transition wasn't immediate; it developed over time as the lesson of exile.

~

On July 20, 2016, three months after receiving the Aurora Prize, Maggy celebrated her sixtieth birthday. Her friends threw her a party. I was in Kigali at the time, and Maggy invited me to join the celebration. Bob Rugurika was there. Richard Nijimbere was there. Lydia and Lysette were there, along with many other people who as children had been the beneficiaries of Maison Shalom. The house where we gathered was also filled with countless recent refugees, like the women who had sewn Maggy's clothes and many other Burundians who had been living in exile for years in Europe and the United States.

The celebration was accompanied by sorrow, and by a reminder of how precarious life had become for Burundians. Two weeks earlier, Bosco Niganze, one of the former children of Maison Shalom whom Maggy held especially close, had been killed in Burundi. Early in the war, Catholic missionaries had delivered Bosco to Maggy after his whole family had been killed near the Congo border. He was five or six, and they couldn't find a home for him because he was blind, not from birth but from the trauma of witnessing his family's murder.

Bosco grew up in Maison Shalom, and his salvation turned out to be music. He learned to play the guitar and became an accomplished musician. When Maggy turned fifty-five, he wrote her a song and sang it at her birthday party. He had let Maggy know that he was working on a new song for her sixtieth birthday and planned to come to Rwanda to sing it at her party. He didn't make it. "He was killed by the government," Maggy said. "They followed him and killed him in a simulated accident. His songs were sometimes critical of the government, but they killed him also to make me suffer."

One of her birthday gifts was a framed photograph of a young Maggy with a baby in her arms; beneath it were words from the Book of Esther: "For such a time as this." Maggy, her friends proclaimed, was Burundi's Esther. In the biblical story, Esther is a Jewish woman who becomes queen to the Persian king Xerxes I, the same Xerxes known for overrunning ancient Greece in the battles of Thermopylae, Salamis, and Plataea in the fifth century BCE. Xerxes does not know that Esther is Jewish, and he has been manipulated into a decree that will lead to the deaths of all Jews in the kingdom. Having learned of Xerxes's intent to kill all the Jews, Esther's cousin Mordecai tells her that she must confront Xerxes: "Who knows? Perhaps you have come to royal dignity for just such a time as this" (Esther 4:14).

Maggy accepted the comparison, just as she had accepted the comparison to Joseph a year earlier when Lydia used the Joseph story to encourage her to flee Burundi. Joseph's brothers sold him into slavery, but years later, having found favor with Pharaoh, he was able to save Israel from famine. "God sent me before you to preserve for you a remnant on earth and to keep alive for you many survivors. So it was not you who sent me here but God" (Genesis 45:7–8). Maggy calls what happened to Joseph the "mistake" that saved his people. Nkurunziza, she says, made the same mistake when he attempted to kill her. In her first year of exile, speaking of her work in Rwanda with Burundian refugees, Maggy said, "I discovered that I have a new mission, not only for orphans but to be the leader of a people."

Biblical allusions for Maggy's life abound: Esther, Joseph, Jonah, Mary, the widow from Zarephath. Once in 2015, before her exile, Maggy compared herself to "old Samuel." It was old Samuel who anointed young David king and then died a short time later, with the work God had given him complete. "If I die today, I think my mission is finished. I admire what God has achieved through a little woman like me. I don't know how to explain it. Sometimes now when I cry, I cry of joy. We have suffered so much—but to see Dieudonné today, to see Richard, to see Lysette, to see what my children have become. I am like the old Samuel in the Bible."

Three months after her birthday party in Kigali, Maggy found herself giving a talk in Malmö, Sweden, in which she invoked a biblical parallel of a different kind. She was there at the invitation of the Vatican, one of four people providing testimony to faith in hard times as part of a joint Catholic–Lutheran commemoration of the five hundredth anniversary of the Reformation.

I watched Maggy's talk on her phone. She had pulled up the clip of a grainy video someone had created by recording their television screen during the broadcast of the event. It showed Maggy in a large sports arena that had been converted into a venue for a papal audience. She was standing on stage like a rock star, a microphone arcing from her ear to her mouth. A large screen in the background was flashing pictures of her work in Burundi. The pope and other dignitaries were seated behind her, off to the side of the stage. Speaking slowly, sometimes spacing her words for dramatic effect, she was describing how she had created Maison Shalom to welcome suffering children.

"Everybody said to me, 'What are you doing? Are you crazy? We are in a war, you have no money.' I said, 'Those children are . . . our . . . future, are . . . our . . . hope.'" When she landed on *hope*, the arena broke into applause. As that died down, she continued to recite what she had said to her detractors. "Don't forget . . . that the first . . . crazy man . . . was . . . Jesus." That last word came out an octave higher than the others, like she was springing a surprise.

More applause followed, and the camera panned to Pope Francis, catching him in a smile, the kind that starts small and then grows. Maggy didn't have a clip of his address on her phone, but she told me that in his remarks the pope had referred to hers. Later I found the address he gave on the occasion: "You said that everybody who knows you thinks what you are doing is crazy. Of course, it is the craziness of love for God and our neighbor. We need more of this craziness. I am grateful that even now, in exile, you continue to spread a message of peace."[25]

~

Maggy has always been quick to locate her life in the Bible, but in 2017, a few months into her third year of exile, I noticed a subtle shift in her biblical references. In September, she paid me an impromptu visit. She had arrived early for an event at the Carter Center in Atlanta and was looking for something to do. I was only a one-hour flight away.

One evening I was showing Maggy photographs I had taken in the Democratic Republic of the Congo in 2015, in the village of a mutual friend not that far north from the border with Burundi. In 2002, during the war that unfolded in DRC after the Rwandan genocide, militias had massacred twelve hundred residents in the village and then occupied it for more than a year. When they finally moved on, they left behind buildings without doors, windows, and roofing. My photographs showed those buildings—houses, a school, a pharmacy, a hospital—after eleven years of exposure to the elements of a tropical climate. The brick structures had become shells melting back into the jungle. I was scrolling through the photographs when Maggy made me pause.

I could see her making the connection to what she had left behind in Burundi—the swimming pool, the movie theater, the library, the maternity center . . . the hospital. She may even have been thinking back to the ruins of the single-story hotel she had reclaimed for offices and vocational training as part of the City of Angels. When she bought the lot, the building's roof was gone, its doors and windows were missing, and weeds and blackberry bushes had overtaken the interior of its rooms. She was no stranger to what vandalism paired with a tropical climate will do to abandoned buildings.

Fourteen months earlier, when I met Maggy in Kigali after her escape from Burundi, I asked, "How do you think about what you left behind? For more than twenty years Maison Shalom was building, building, building. You couldn't have imagined it would end this way. It must be devastating." Maggy laughed. "No. Because for me the buildings were not important. I wasn't working to build buildings. I was distributing love and happiness. I've lost nothing. Maison Shalom was born in the heart of God. It is a message, not something made of brick."

Years later I would hear Maggy make the same point differently. In April 2019, a fire devastated Notre-Dame de Paris, the famous medieval cathedral in France. "You've seen what happened at Notre-Dame in Paris," Maggy said. "I received telephone calls from rich families in Paris, and they were crying and crying. I asked, 'How many people died?' and they said, 'Nobody died.' Imagine, all those tears, and no one died. In my country, in 2021, a fire in Gitega prison killed four hundred people. In Paris, they should have been celebrating that nobody died."

About what she left behind in Burundi, Maggy says, "I have never put importance in things that are brick. I've never cried over the buildings, just the babies who were in the hospital. Twenty-one babies were in the hospital when the government ceased our funding and Richard had to flee. I only cried for the babies."

That said, I've seen Maggy cry over buildings, however briefly, while staring at pictures of a village disappearing into the foliage of a Congolese rainforest. The moment stood out, not only because Maggy does not cry easily but because it was accompanied by what seemed to be a deepening awareness that her own exile and that of her people could last for a long, long time, which put in question who they would be when they returned, what they would return to, and how they should live in the meantime.

What I noticed when Maggy visited me in 2017 was the frequency of her biblical allusions. It was as if the Bible was no longer simply a reference for her life; instead, her life had effectively collapsed into the biblical narrative, which at its core is a story of exile and return. Adam and Eve were exiles from Eden. Cain became a fugitive and wanderer. Abraham left his home for an unknown land. A famine brought all of Israel to Egypt, where their status as refugees became permanent until the Exodus. It was as refugees that Israel wandered in the wilderness and crossed the Jordan into the promised land, but not before Moses warned them that they could easily become refugees again, which came to pass when the Babylonians carried the people away into another exile. And so on and so on—right up to the time that Mary, Joseph, and Jesus became refugees: "Get up, take the child and his mother, and flee to Egypt" (Matthew 2:13).

The theme of exile and return is everywhere in the biblical narrative, even in the recesses of the primary drama, as when Ruth leaves her home to accompany Naomi as she returns to hers. Apt comparisons for Maggy's life now included Ezekiel, the prophet of exile; Ezra, who led his people back to Israel after seventy years in Babylon; and Nehemiah, who, when the people returned, led the rebuilding of Jerusalem. What caught my eye in 2017 was the way Maggy's life in exile had opened seemingly endless possibilities of comparison to the biblical narrative, but it was also something else.

Maggy herself had become a biblical character. "I don't think there is a person like me who has seen so many bad things and so many amazing things." It's that combination of suffering and joy, both experienced in unimaginable depth, not once or twice but over a lifetime, that makes Maggy biblical.

~

When Maggy visited me in 2017, she was well into her second year of turning Maison Shalom into a Rwandan organization focused on refugees, most of whom were from Burundi. After arriving in Rwanda in June 2015, she had not wasted time. Maison Shalom received its license to operate as a nongovernmental organization in Rwanda in September. Richard became director in November, after his own flight from Burundi. By the end of December, more than seventy thousand Burundians had registered with UNHCR as refugees. Of those, almost forty-five thousand were living in the camp Rwanda had established in Mahama, four hours east of Kigali on the Tanzanian border.[26]

The camp quickly became the primary focus of Maison Shalom's work. "When I fled Burundi, they thought I would give up. They had attacked me. They had condemned me. They thought the bad experience would cause me to say, 'I'm done. I will stay in Luxembourg.' But to see my people in such a way, I had to join them, and I said to God, 'Come with me.'"

I toured the camp with Maggy in July 2016. Many of the refugees in the camp had been living there for more than a year. At the end of March and the beginning of April 2015, as many as five hundred people a day were fleeing from Burundi into Rwanda and registering as refugees. That was the official count and included only people in dire need of assistance. On April 17, the government of Rwanda allocated land for the camp. It opened five days later with a population of almost ten thousand refugees.

A staff member from UNHCR remembers the moment: "When we came to register the refugees in the first week of the camp, there was no construction, there were no facilities for water, and there were so many refugees it was in a serious emergency condition. Because of the huge numbers of refugees, we put up large communal shelters and prepared hot meals, just to ensure people had basic support in the first days."[27] On our tour of the camp, I met the camp planner, a Kenyan working for UNHCR. He had a master's degree in humanitarian practice. I asked him if anything he'd learned was a help in setting up the camp. "No," he said. "I'm not sure anything could prepare you for the chaos generated by that much immediate need."

A report from UNHCR on April 28, two days after the protests erupted in Bujumbura and just the seventh day of the camp's existence, deepens the description: "Over the weekend, the number of Burundian refugees crossing into Rwanda has jumped significantly, with over 5,000 refugees entering the country in just two days. Since the beginning of April, nearly 21,000 Burundians, mostly women and children, have fled to Rwanda. UNHCR and its partners are moving refugees to the new Mahama refugee camp in daily convoys of up to 1,500 people."[28]

The report went on to note that UNHCR had already erected more than 450 family tents and that another 1,000 were expected by the end of the day. The official capacity of a UNHCR family tent is five people, but UNCHR nearly doubled that number and projected that these tents would accommodate almost 13,000 refugees. The population of the camp on May 13, three weeks after it opened, was 21,096 and had already outstripped even this stretching of capacity.

When I visited the camp, the population had grown to 50,000, and it was a sea of worn-out UNHCR tents being replaced slowly by small stick and mud houses and an occasional home constructed of hand-made, unfired brick—all sitting on a desolate landscape of dusty red clay. The tents, one next to another at haphazard angles, spread out down a gentle hill into a wide ravine and then sloped up another hill—as far as the eye could see. The hilly ground sloped into the Kagera River, which forms the border between Rwanda and Tanzania.

At the time, Maison Shalom was still getting traction in the camp. With children making up more than 50 percent of the population—ten thousand of them between the ages of five and eleven—the work focused mostly on education, often by placing older children in boarding schools. Additional efforts included shoring up health care by training women in the camp to function as community health workers, educating and supporting pregnant women and young mothers. These activities, however, were not the most fundamental thing Maison Shalom was offering refugees. That came in the form of another celebration of Maggy's birthday during which Maggy, Richard, and Lysette each offered their own stories to the refugees as words of encouragement and hope.

Richard's story was especially fitting. He showed them the scars on his arms from the burns he received when the table he was hiding under caught fire. He told them of his time in a camp in Tanzania just like this one. And he offered himself as proof of a future beyond the camp. Later he told me that one of the saddest things he had ever experienced was meeting someone in the Mahama camp that he had known more than twenty years earlier in a camp in Tanzania.

After our tour, I found myself trying to imagine Maggy's first visit to the camp. Even a year later, with resources and a semblance of order, the need and desperation were overwhelming. Where would one have started in July 2015? With that question in mind, I asked, "What's the first thing you did?" On her phone, she showed me a video from one of her early visits to the camp; it showed people singing and dancing. "When I first saw the camp, it hurt me. I couldn't sleep. And I said, 'I must transform this camp. I must follow my vocation.' The only vocation, the human vocation, is to distribute happiness and life, which comes straight from God. Not the life they impose on us, all those ideologies. To start, I said, 'Go, celebrate, just be the ambassador of happiness.'"

When we returned to Kigali, we stopped at Maison Shalom's sparsely furnished office: two desks piled with binders and papers; a cloth-draped table holding a computer and printer; a single file cabinet; and one lone picture on the bare walls— Maggy meeting Pope Benedict. "This one is special," she said. "It's from 2009, when the pope invited me to talk to all the African bishops. He had gathered them in Rome for a synod on the church in Africa. I was the only woman to speak."

The theme of the synod, Maggy explained, was focused on reconciliation, justice, and peace. She thought the bishops fell short. "I said to the pope, 'Holy Father, I must tell you, there are no Christians in Africa. They are baptized, but the bishops didn't talk about orphans, child soldiers, children in the streets, refugees, not even Sudan. They didn't even mention Darfur." Maggy's summary of the synod turned to laughter when she reported what one of the bishops had said to her after she criticized them directly: "You are really a punishment that God sent to us."

Maggy had a similar conversation with Pope John Paul II when, remarkably, he made a three-day visit to Burundi in September 1990. "I was in a Catholic school in 1972 during the genocide against Hutu, and all these years later Hutu and Tutsi continued to fight, even though we say we are all one family and in Burundi we were 80 percent Catholic. I decided I wanted to meet the pope." Maggy approached the apostolic nunciature to request an audience with John Paul II, not for her alone but for a group of young Burundians. "We wanted to express our disagreement with the bishops in Burundi, with their refusal to denounce ethnic hatred and violence." In retrospect, Maggy sees the boldness of her request and laughs when she describes meeting the pope.

"I said to him, 'It's like a mother who is a prostitute. You can't hate your mother, even when she's a prostitute. She's still your mother. In Burundi, my mother church, the Catholic Church, is missing her mission. Because of that I will love her more. You can't abandon your mother when she is ill. You must take care of her." Maggy ends the story by saying, "He listened to me when I said, 'I will never accept that my mother has become a prostitute.'"

~

The day after we visited the Mahama camp and made the stop at the office, Maggy took me to see the start of her next big dream. She had recently leased a collection of buildings that had been a hotel and restaurant, and she had begun to turn it into the Oasis of Peace, an urban center for refugees. In addition to the tens of thousands of refugees Rwanda was harboring in camps like Mahama, thousands more were congregating in Kigali. The Oasis of Peace was Maggy's response.

She was planning to restart the restaurant to generate income and as a vehicle for culinary training for refugees, alongside other vocational programs. She also intended for the Oasis of Peace to serve as a cultural center for a people in exile. One of the challenges she had already identified was that, in just a few years, young children from Burundi could lose both their Kirundi and French language skills—the only two languages spoken with any regularity in Burundi. In Rwanda, after third grade, French and Kinyarwanda (close to Kirundi) had moved from the languages of instruction to electives, and all classes were taught in English. Even in 2016, she was starting to plan for an exile that could last a long time.

Three years later, a long exile seemed almost assured, as did continued suffering for those unable or unwilling to flee from Burundi. In June 2019, Maggy addressed Canada's parliament and described life in Burundi under Nkurunziza's continued rule:

Children are suffering from malnutrition. People are starving to death. Burundi has become an open-air prison. We had demobilized 1,500 child soldiers and helped them rebuild their lives. However, Burundi has just recruited 60,000 young militiamen from the ruling party, who are known as the *Imbonerakure*. They scour all the hills and instigate terror, violence, and death with an air of complete indifference. Many young girls are now being sold. Young boys are being tortured and castrated. Of the 500,000 Burundians in exile, 60% are malnourished children. What will happen to all these children? If these children have no hope, they'll take up arms. You'll see them again when they become child soldiers and it will be too late. Pierre Nkurunziza, the President of the Republic, has become a fascist. It's a fascist regime. I'm now standing here like a mother who's crying out for something to be done before it's too late.[29]

Meanwhile, in the Mahama refugee camp and in Kigali Maggy was doing what she could through Maison Shalom and the Oasis of Peace to help her people survive an exile of unknown duration by preparing them for their return to Burundi, not as rebels, which had often been the African model, but as carpenters and tailors, doctors and lawyers, and all the rest. "I laugh," she says, "because they tried to bury us, but they forgot that we are seeds."

PART THREE

Return

I will restore your fortunes and gather you from all the nations and all the places where I have driven you, says the Lord, and I will bring you back to the place from which I sent you into exile.

I am going to gather them from the farthest parts of the earth, among them the blind and the lame, those with child and those in labor together; a great company, they shall return here. With weeping they shall come, and with consolations I will lead them back. Then shall the young women rejoice in the dance, and the young men and the old shall be merry. There is hope for your future, your children shall come back to their own country.

—Jeremiah 29:14; 31:8–9, 13, 17

In July 2024, I traveled to Rwanda for a set of closing conversations with Maggy in preparation for the final draft of this book. We had not seen one another since April 2022, and that visit had come after a pandemic-stretched gap of four-and-a-half years. Before traveling, I worked with Maggy to arrange the trip. I would come for ten days. She would show me the work of Maison Shalom in Kigali. We would make the trip to Mahama. And we would have ample time for conversation. All of this would allow me to pick up her story where I had left it back in 2022, just before her cancer diagnosis.

Twice before, I had arranged what I thought were final conversations with Maggy that would lead to a finale of sorts, to some closing scene. Before exile, that scene was of Maggy retreating from Maison Shalom. "If the security is good, I will return to my village when I turn sixty." In exile, the scene had changed. "They tried to bury us, but they forgot that we are seeds." I went to Rwanda in July 2024 wondering what scene would emerge this time. What artificial but necessary stopping point would I find in telling the story of a life? How would the story end?

What I discovered is that a global pandemic, a cancer diagnosis, and an exile of almost a decade—all wrapped up in a life—make for a complicated story. Maggy may have become a biblical character caught up in a story of exile and return, but when the resolution of return does not include going home, what shape does the story take?

～

The end of exile flashed briefly on June 8, 2020, when Pierre Nkurunziza died suddenly at the age of fifty-five. The government reported his official cause of death as a heart attack, but it's likely that he died from COVID-19. His wife was flown to Nairobi on May 28 for emergency medical care and hospitalized with the virus.[1] His death came two months before the end of his third term as president, the one he had acquired through violence and intimidation and that had led hundreds of thousands of his people to flee the country. It's tempting to wonder in a whimsical way if Maggy might have had something to do with his death. "I prayed for him," Maggy said of her meeting with him in 2014, "but in an angry way: 'God, please take him quickly.'" Maggy herself, however, now looks back at her feelings toward Nkurunziza and sees them as a misplaced vortex of emotion that pulled her into anger and thoughts of violence that run counter to her deep commitment to peace.

Having already served a questionable third term, Nkurunziza did not seek a fourth. Instead he endorsed the candidacy of Évariste Ndayishimiye, who won the May election, and then, because of Nkurunziza's death, assumed office two months early. Among Ndayishimiye's first acts was to invite Burundian refugees to come home. Some returned, but most stayed away, waiting for signs of real change, which failed to come.

One human rights report summarizing Ndayishimiye's first year and a half in power concluded, "Many of Ndayishimiye's repeated promises to deliver justice and promote political tolerance remain unfulfilled." The report described what unfulfilled promises look like: "killings, disappearances, torture, ill-treatment, arbitrary arrests and detention, and sexual and gender-based violence."[2] Not surprising news to Maggy. During the war, Ndayishimiye and Nkurunziza were both leaders in the CNDD-FDD, the Hutu rebel group that formed in the first year of the war and became the ruling political party when the war ended.

What did come as a surprise was the news that, shortly before Nkurunziza's death, the Supreme Court of Burundi heard charges against Maggy and eleven other Burundians in exile, and that, shortly after his death, all twelve were convicted and sentenced to *une peine de prison à perpétuité*—which in Maggy's English becomes "a life of perpetual prison." Laughing, she adds, "plus twenty years." Among the twelve people charged and convicted in absentia for their alleged participation in the events of April and May 2015, Maggy alone received that extra twenty years. "Apparently, they want to punish me in the next life too."

Maggy, Bob Rugurika, and ten others were prosecuted specifically for having "directly taken part in the execution and/or directly cooperated in the execution of the attack whose aim was to change the constitutional regime and to incite citizens to arm themselves against the authority of the State; assassinated soldiers, police officers and civilians; wickedly destroyed and damaged several buildings."[3]

The Supreme Court heard the charges on April 28, six weeks before Nkurunziza's death, and returned their judgment on June 23, two weeks into Ndayishimiye's presidency, leaving little doubt about continuity in the transition from one regime to the other. Neither the charges nor the conviction and sentencing became public until February 2021, when Maggy, like everyone else, learned of it through social media.

The illegal conviction and the life sentence had no practical effect on Maggy, other than to underscore the need for a life of caution. She doesn't travel in Africa outside Rwanda, fearing that one of the other African governments might give her up. She travels freely in Canada, the United States, and Europe, though she had one close call in Istanbul. And when traveling on planes and through airports, she no longer wears the colorful dresses and head wraps that had long been her signatures.

Within Rwanda, she also became more careful. As the grand duchess reminded her, Burundi is nearby. From Kigali to the border is under a hundred miles by road. From Mahama to the border is far less. Maggy never rides in the front seat, rarely goes out after dark, and surrounds herself with people she trusts, those she has known for a long time, mostly former children of Maison Shalom. "There are always people, intelligence agencies . . ." Maggy pauses. "It's why you have seen that the workers, the people who prepare my food for example, are my former children. You have met Rose, in the kitchen. She came to Maison Shalom as a teenager in 1995 after surviving a massacre in Gitega. Even in Mahama, you have seen that it is my former children who prepare the food."

~

The transition from Pierre Nkurunziza to Évariste Ndayishimiye may have had no real effect on Maggy, but the pandemic taking place at the same time presented a whole new field of possibility for love and invention. During the early months of the pandemic, the Rwandan ministry in charge of refugees put all the camps in lockdown and scaled back to only essential services. Maison Shalom was no longer allowed to work in the camp, which had reached its maximum capacity of sixty thousand refugees.[4]

According to the rules of the lockdown, refugees in the camp, normally free to come and go at will, could leave for only two activities: building and cultivating. At the time, Maison Shalom was heavily invested in education, and their primary method was to pay for students to attend schools outside the camp. These efforts included supporting older students to attend universities. Suddenly no one, not even the students, could leave the camp except to build or cultivate. "So," Maggy says, laughing, "we built and we cultivated."

What to build came quickly to Maggy. "I was thinking about the staff of aid organizations like Save the Children. They don't like to live nearby in Mahama. It's poor, with no facilities, so they live fifty kilometers away. That's how they spend their per diems. I was thinking, 'How can I keep them here, so they don't arrive at noon, stay a few hours, and then go back?' And I said, 'I'll build a restaurant, and they can pay Maison Shalom. And all those young people in the camp can build it and then be the staff. It could be vocational training.'"

Following this logic, Maggy employed refugees to build not only a restaurant in Mahama right next to the camp, but also a hotel and facilities to house vocational training centers for trades like carpentry, culinary arts, hairdressing, and cobbling.

At the same time, she turned her attention to cultivation. "I bought twenty hectares, and ten thousand pangas, and said to the people in the camp, 'Okay. Come, work. Bring everybody.' They could leave the camp, cultivate, and earn something. Five thousand refugees registered to leave the camp. They would go to the fields in the morning and come back in the evening, singing . . ." Maggy pauses to underscore the scale. "Five thousand refugees." She also explains that all this cultivation overlapped with the World Food Programme's announcement in February 2021 that it was cutting its food aid to refugees in Rwanda by 60 percent.[5]

By the time the pandemic ended, Maison Shalom had been transformed. I asked Maggy about that transformation in April 2022, when she came to Duke for an invited lecture that had been postponed for two years because of the pandemic. "If I were to come visit today, what would I see?" She answered:

> In Kigali, at Oasis of Peace, we have our offices, with sixty-seven employees, and we have a restaurant and culinary training and a nursery school, and we give loans and provide training in entrepreneurship, and we have a cultural center. We perform plays and project films, and I dream of a cinema. In the camp, no tents. Everybody lives in a house. We have a learning center, vocational training for sewing and for computers, and a library, and we continue to sponsor children to go to boarding schools and university. Outside the camp, we have twenty hectares. We have cows. We have pigs. We have chickens. And we cultivate tea. It's a cooperative. Now people leave the camp in the morning, singing, to work in the fields. And we have a restaurant and a small hotel and hairdressing and the culinary arts, and I ordered machines from India for making shoes.

She didn't end this list by saying, "It is like that," but it was rhythmically implied. Instead, she paused before saying, "Perhaps I will build another hospital, and I will call it Rema."

~

The transformation of Maison Shalom since Maggy reestablished it in Rwanda in 2015 has not been limited to a pandemic-assisted expansion of infrastructure and programs for refugees in Mahama and Kigali. It has also been missional. Maison Shalom is now Maison Shalom International, with the mission "to see every human being live with dignity and flourish fully in any society."[6] This mission follows from Maggy's own transformation, one that's been underway since she was on stage receiving the Aurora Prize in 2016 and found herself caught up in two different emotions.

On one hand, the award gave her the courage and strength to live in exile with the hope that one day she would return to Burundi and sing its national anthem: "Our Burundi, sacred heritage from our forefathers / worthy of our tenderest love, we vow to your noble service our hands and hearts and lives." On the other hand, the award was the sign she had asked for, confirmation that God was calling her to something new, something beyond her commitment to Burundi: "a humanitarian award to awaken humanity, and for me to be the first . . ."

Since 2016, Maggy's life has been a display of what those two emotions become if they develop into close companions instead of conflicting commitments. Early on, Maggy's interpretation of her new role was not as expansive as it would become. Explaining the impact of the Aurora Prize to me just a few months after receiving the award, she said, "I discovered that I had a new mission. To create hope for everybody. At first, I was a little shy, but now I have decided to arrange interviews, to attend conferences in Europe, to go to the UN and denounce what is happening in my country. I have seen the sign of God.

I have had a prophecy. I cannot stay in indifference. My people are dying, are killed every day. I must protest. We suffer so much."

Without doubt, Maggy understood the Aurora Prize to be the sign of a new mission: *to create hope for everybody*. But when Maggy went on the road, her concern for the people of Burundi remained the driving force and the focus of her message. The members of Canada's parliament heard it clearly when she addressed them in 2019: "Children are suffering from malnutrition. People are starving to death. Burundi has become an open-air prison. . . . I'm now standing here like a mother who's crying out for something to be done before it's too late."

The message sounded different in 2021 when Maggy reported on the work of Maison Shalom, thanking those whose generosity had made its programs in Rwanda possible: "Soon seven years of exile, seven years of learning a new life, seven years of mourning. And here we are. Still standing up for our dignity. We fled leaving everything behind us, traumatized, tortured, raped, some of us unjustly sentenced to life in prison. Dear friends, your faith in Maison Shalom has put us back on the path of our vocation to humanize humanity."[7] Everything from 2016 was still there but with a new endgame.

As Maggy and Maison Shalom emerged from the pandemic with a refined message, Maggy started to see that she faced an organizational challenge. Was it in fact Maison Shalom's vocation to humanize humanity, or was it hers? Even with the addition of "International" to its name, Maison Shalom remained an organization focused entirely on its work with refugees in Rwanda, and on the crises in Burundi and Congo that had turned "camps" like Mahama into seemingly permanent settlements. Maggy worked through this organizational challenge in conversation with François Mairlot, a longtime friend in Belgium.

～

François and Maggy met in 2004, through François's wife, Véronique. In May that year, Maggy received an honorary degree from Université catholique de Louvain in Belgium. Véronique's father was on the university's board of trustees. He heard Maggy speak and called his daughter. "You must meet this woman." Véronique called Maggy to set up a meeting for the next month when Maggy planned to come to back to Brussels with some of her kids who needed medical care.

By 2004, this kind of trip had become routine for Maggy. The flights and medical care were arranged by generous people who had either met her in Burundi or encountered her work through magazines or documentaries. Sometimes the journalist who wrote the story arranged the care. That's how Maggy got Dieudonné, the baby she had plucked from his mother's back in Butezi, to Germany for reconstructive surgery. Often, what wasn't arranged for such trips was where Maggy would stay. "Always I had problems because I had no money to go to a hotel."

Maggy's solution was to ask Burundian families living abroad if she could stay with them, but that wasn't always possible. "It was difficult to go to a Tutsi family when I had a Hutu child because they didn't accept that I had denounced Tutsi violence and that Hutu kids also had suffered and been mutilated. Sometimes, I would try to hide my Hutu children. It was also difficult to go to a Hutu family with a Tutsi child. Sometimes when I stayed with these Burundian families it caused conflict, and the police would even come."

When Maggy returned to Brussels as planned in June 2004, her lodging situation caused complications for her meeting with Véronique. She was staying in a touch-and-go place that turned out to be close to Véronique and François's home, and Véronique proposed that she pick up Maggy there. "I didn't want her to see where I was staying and for her to learn about my problems. I said, 'Yes, you can come. I will meet you outside with my suitcase and we can go quickly.'" Despite this effort, Véronique learned of Maggy's issues with housing and said, "It doesn't matter, you can always come to my home."

Brussels was the transit for Maggy's flights out of Africa, and she accepted Véronique's offer. "I think because of my faith," Maggy says, "always when I have a challenge, when I have so many problems, God sends me an angel. I can say it, loudly, that after I met Véronique so many of my anxieties went away. For me travel was so stressful. I was traumatized. Sometimes I had to sleep in the airport, waiting for the next flight, with no money and wounded kids; one might be missing a hand, one a mouth, and another with no eyes. And everybody looked at me without compassion." That all changed with Véronique and François. Since 2004 they have welcomed Maggy into their home so often that she has become part of the family. "Véronique," Maggy says, "is really my little sister."

The date Maggy first met Véronique and François is another of the fixed dates in Maggy's story: June 8, 2004. I thought perhaps the date was memorable because of a Catholic feast day or some other event of significance in Maggy's life, but when I asked why she remembered the date so clearly, she said simply, "Because it changed my life. They took my cross. They became like Simon in the Bible."

François describes Maggy's visits by saying, "When she's in the house, I don't have to ask if she's there because of the noise of her laughter." He remembers clearly the first time Véronique brought her home:

It was a moment of my life when I was questioning humanity. We didn't have the best people ruling the world—as is still the case today—and I was very disappointed by what I was seeing. Suddenly this person pops out of nowhere. She had passed through a difficult and dark time, but she was shining; she was laughing, being optimistic about her unrealistic dreams. But at the end of the day, she managed to succeed, which for a business-man like me is hard to understand. Her business plan has three parts: love, love, and love. Strangely enough, it works. She has been a candle in the night.[8]

What François has always found most compelling about Maggy are not the accomplishments of Maison Shalom, as notable as those are, but the way she shows up as an answer to deep disappointments in humanity. It's not surprising, there-fore, that as he watched Maggy's life in exile expand her voca-tion he proposed that she create a new organization. What she needed, he suggested, was a platform for the work God handed her when he sent the sign that came in the form of an award for awakening humanity.

The Fondation Maggy Barankitse was established in Febru-ary 2021. Located in Belgium, its primary mission is "to raise awareness, as widely as possible, for the universal message car-ried by Marguerite Barankitse, namely, 'humanizing human-ity through love, compassion, and resilience in action.'" The foundation's secondary mission is "to support the field actions developed by Maison Shalom International."[9] The creation of the Belgian foundation surfaced a critical question about the relationship between Maggy and Maison Shalom. Maggy had put that question in play before her exile, when everything was still running smoothly in Burundi and she was thinking about where her life was headed.

～

The first time Maggy told me of her hopes for the future, we were together in Uganda. It was mid-January 2015, the week after her failed attempt to convince the archbishop in Burundi to meet with Nkurunziza and just days before the arrest of Bob Rugurika. Fittingly, given where my conversations with Maggy had started years earlier, she talked of her hopes for the future in response to a question I had asked her about traditional burial practices in Burundi.

"I'm wondering," I said, "as you've thought through the morgue and the care of the dead, how much you are drawing on your traditional practices and not Christian practices." My query was prompted by a comment Maggy had made about the traditional Burundian practice of burying family members just outside the home and planting a tree on the grave. "For me it's both," she said. "Good things from both must stay. Like Jesus said, 'I've come not to abolish but to perfect.'"

I asked her to say more about the practice of burying the dead outside the home. She replied, "For me that's important, because cemeteries make no sense in our tradition. Of course, I'm Christian, but it's unfortunate that when the missionaries came, they undermined our burial practices. In Burundi, people don't respect cemeteries, which is why I always go to work on the *tombe*. No one goes there to take care of it." I clarified her drift into French, "*Tombe?* You mean the mass grave?"

"Yes," she said, and then explained that her mother was buried in a different cemetery, the one where she and the children went to hide in 1993. That cemetery was also unkempt and overgrown with grass and weeds because no one in Burundi visits cemeteries. "I have taken my mom from the cemetery and brought her to the village where I will live. I will plant a tree on her grave. And I will put in my last testament that I, too, want to stay in my village after I die. I have already built my house. If the security is good, I will return to my village when I turn sixty in July 2016 and retreat from Maison Shalom. I want Richard to take it."

That's how things looked in January 2015, when the events that cascaded Maggy into exile were just over the horizon. At the time, all was not well in Burundi and Maggy was keeping an eye on security. Nonetheless, her plans were for retirement, not exile, and Richard was well-positioned to take over Maison Shalom, which Maggy had shaped in the same way as the *Fratrie*.

Just as the houses Maison Shalom had built for children belonged to them, Maison Shalom itself effectively belonged to the staff, 75 percent of whom were its own former orphans. In a sense, Maggy had built a succession plan into the very fabric of the organization, and she had spent years preparing Richard to take over leadership. But between her escape in June and Richard's flight in November, all that fell apart in 2015.

Before her exile, Maggy and Maison Shalom were poised for separation, and it was possible to imagine Maggy without Maison Shalom as she retreated to her village on Nyamutobo Hill. It was equally possible to imagine Maison Shalom without Maggy as Richard and countless other former orphans carried on what she had started and energized for more than two decades. After exile, however, Maggy and Maison Shalom collapsed back into one another.

The creation of the foundation in Belgium in 2021 provided Maggy a new avenue for separation, not with retirement in view but as a vehicle for her vocation of awakening humanity. However, before she could take advantage of this new platform, she was diagnosed with breast cancer.

～

Ironically, Maggy's status as a refugee saved her life. Regular medical care had not been part of Maggy's routines, but Luxembourg's health insurance required that she have a physical at sixty-five. That's when they caught the cancer. Maggy informed me of her diagnosis in a WhatsApp message.

I had texted her on April 29, 2022, a few weeks after she had visited Duke. I was finishing up an early draft of this book and had asked her one of my lingering questions. The usual prompt reply didn't come. Then on May 10, this message arrived: "Dear

David, I am so sorry for this delay to answer. In French they say, *l'homme propose et Dieu dispose*. It has taken time because I have been diagnosed with breast cancer. But as you know, I will still stand up and fight. I am in Kigali to prepare everything and return to Luxembourg for six months of treatment."

In mid-June, I texted Maggy for an update. She replied, "I am on my third chemo. As you know my life has always been a fight. I won all those fights thanks to divine love. Together with all the friends God has given to me, we will make the impossible possible. Don't be afraid my dearest, I think this cancer is a divine message that I must let others take care of me. God is God. His name is love."

Another message followed, this one accompanied by photographs of Maggy's caregivers and various friends visiting her in Luxembourg: "Nothing changes with me. Life is a feast. Together with all the friends that God gave to me, we will make the impossible possible. I am blessed with all the generosity of all my friends. They are taking turns staying with me here at the Franciscan convent where I live while I am in treatment."

Later I would learn that the grand duchess had suggested that Maggy stay with her during treatment, but, Maggy said, "I didn't want to live in a palace, so I rented a room in the convent. During seven months, I spent many hours in the chapel, praying. And it was so full of grace. I discovered a new phase of life. My treatment made me helpless like a baby. Nurses had to give me medicine and wash me. This gave me humility. And then I discovered the beauty of life."

Being forced to let others care for her allowed Maggy to encounter God in a new way, through care and companionship. "I was never alone," she says. "Lysette came with Lydia for three months. Mia came from Texas. An African priest came to celebrate Mass for me in the hospital. The queen came to visit. I always had a list of who was coming next, and in the hospital, everyone was saying, 'Who is this woman?'"

One of Maggy's visitors during her treatment was an old friend from Burundi who had moved to Luxembourg. Her photograph had been in one of Maggy's WhatsApp messages, but only later did I hear the accompanying story. She was one of Maggy's Hutu classmates in 1972 when her father was killed in the genocide that launched Maggy into a teaching career. "We were both sixteen," Maggy says. "She lost her father but said nothing. I said to her, 'Why must you hide? They killed your father, and you don't want to tell me? But I also suffer from the loss of my father, who died naturally. You, you can't bear it because you don't know what happened to your father, where they took him.' And then we cried together." Now, fifty years later, this woman came to support Maggy in her time of trial.

As Maggy's cancer treatment progressed, I checked in with her now and again, and she usually responded in the same positive vein. "I continue to celebrate life. It is a special moment for me. A moment of grace and meditation." The one exception came in late October when she canceled a planned conversation via Zoom. She sent her regrets: "I am so sorry for this evening. I am not good."

In early November, Maggy let me know a scheduled surgery had gone well: "Yesterday my doctor informed me that there is no more cellules cancéreuses. I can return to Rwanda and celebrate Christmas with my children." Photographs from the Kigali airport followed a few weeks later, with a short accompanying note: "I arrived yesterday evening. Too emotional." The photos showed celebratory moments of a homecoming as friends and family greeted Maggy, her characteristic smile doing its best to compete with a pale and gaunt face that revealed the toll of cancer treatment. There must have been many days over the seven months of treatment when Maggy's body compelled her to say, "I am not good."

∼

In early February 2023, Maggy was with one of our mutual friends in Kigali when they decided to give me a call. What transpired over the next thirty-two minutes and five seconds (according to my WhatsApp call log) was the full story of Maggy's cancer, which, it turns out, is the story of what Maggy meant when she had sent text messages saying, "I continue to celebrate life" and "Life is a feast."

Maggy treated the cancer ward in Luxembourg the same way she treated the artillery site on Nyamutobo Hill; the ruins of her village; the abandoned school with its corpses and broken windows; the dumping ground for medical waste next to the government hospital; and the mass grave on the edges of the army camp. Maggy had reconfigured these sites of violence and death into sites of hope. "Nothing changes with me," Maggy said of her cancer treatment, which left only one possibility for the cancer ward in a Luxembourg hospital. Simply by being in it as a patient, Maggy turned the ward into a site of love and life.

When she encountered other women in the ward who were depressed and seemed to have given in to their cancer, she adapted the line she had used when the ambassador's wife found her putting on makeup. "I said, 'Do you want to die before your death?' Then to give hope to those women who were crying in their rooms, I made a fashion show. I distributed colorful cloth to the other women in the ward, and to the nurses, even the doctors. Then we all put on color and paraded down the hallway, singing."

With only a few exceptions, I've never seen Maggy dress in anything other than full-length African dresses that burst with color, accompanied by equally colorful head wraps. She is the epitome of elegance. The one change Maggy made for the fashion shows was to leave behind the head wrap so that her bald head could become part of her beauty. Tuesday was Maggy's day for chemotherapy. Soon everyone wanted their treatments on Tuesdays.

Maggy's refusal to dress in drab hospital gowns persisted even when it came time for surgery. She understood that she could not compromise the aseptic zone of the operating theater, but she was also unwilling to give in to the overarching "sterility" of the hospital environment that she had been combating with her fashion shows. Her solution was to make a deal with the nurses.

She decorated a surgical gown with colorful cloth and brought it to the nurses to be sterilized. Before the surgery, she dressed in the gown, with her fingernail polish and her lipstick. The nurses had agreed to remove everything after anesthesia to prep her for surgery, and to return her to her elegance, lipstick and all, before she came to after the operation. The nurses also accommodated Maggy's request to flood the operating theater with the prayerful music of Gregorian chants. When the surgeon arrived and expressed surprise, the nurses, no longer surprised by anything, simply pointed out that Maggy had transformed the theater into a chapel.

The Gregorian music was not the surgeon's first surprise. When a mastectomy became part of treatment, he met with Maggy to explain the necessity of the procedure. He set his countenance to match what he took to be difficult news and was not ready for Maggy's response: "In Africa, breasts are for feeding babies. I have no babies, and so no need of breasts. You are welcome to take them." Laughter, of course, accompanied her words, and Maggy laughed again when she told the story.

In September 2024, Maggy returned to Luxembourg for a routine follow-up visit with her oncologist. With her scans and bloodwork clear, he removed the catheter in her chest that he had kept in place should she need further therapy. Celebrating the moment, he and the staff who had come to know Maggy during her treatment gave her an envelope that contained five thousand euros. They were always paid for their consultations with cancer patients, they explained, but they had failed to pay

Maggy for her consultation with them. She had transformed their understanding of cancer and of their work, a transformation that had started the moment the oncologist relayed her diagnosis of late-stage breast cancer.

Maggy's response to the oncologist's detailed explanation of her prognosis was laughter. He was confused. "Why are you laughing?" Maggy suggested that they switch chairs because it was clear that he was frightened of death and perhaps she could help him come to terms with his fear. Little did he know then what the next seven months would hold.

Laughter often accompanies Maggy's account of where God was in all this. In one of her text messages, she had said, "God is God. His name is love." But that covers only part of the relationship Maggy has with God. Laughing as she recounts the story of her cancer, she says, "God, why must you always make me suffer and be strong? I can do what I'm doing without the suffering, without losing my hair, without numbness in my fingers and feet, without what chemo is doing to my body."

Maggy stops for context. Still laughing, she says, "It's like that . . . , I pray like that. And sometimes I don't say 'Our Father,' I say 'My Father' because I know it ridicules him. I tell him, 'Today, I will say "My Father" because I do not agree with you. You have a problem with me.'"

Maggy has been arguing with God for a long time—at least since she was on her knees in the bishop's chapel in October 1993 when she was sure that God had lied to her about being a God of love. When she recounts these arguments, she laughs along the way. But when I heard the line "God has a problem with me," I thought immediately of the only other time I had heard her say something like that. On this occasion, too, the topic was suffering and death, but laughter was absent.

~

We were sitting at my dining-room table in April 2022. Her cancer diagnosis was a few weeks in the future, and I was going back over parts of her story, audio recorder on. She was telling me again about the events of October 24, 1993. She had come to the part of the story where the killing had finally ended. "They left and went to kill somewhere in town. And there I was. Among those bodies . . . alone." She followed *alone* with the start of a question, "Can you . . ." She didn't need to finish the sentence for me to answer. "No, I can't imagine."

She started to speak again but stopped after only three words: "And the fire . . ." This time I couldn't finish the sentence, but I knew where the story went from there, so I prompted her to continue: "When you went into the chapel, as I recall, you were angry with God." Maggy spent the next five minutes reciting what happened from the time she entered the chapel thinking her own children were dead to the moment hours later when Martin met her and the children in the cemetery.

When Maggy had finished retelling this part of the story, I asked her something I had never asked before. I recorded her answer earlier, when I was recounting the details of the massacre she witnessed in October 1993. My question was, "How long do you think you were tied in the chair?" Her reply was unhesitating. "One hour, around 10:00, because I can remember the fire, and I can see how I helped one old priest, also a Tutsi, who was trying to save documents. I said, 'You go and hide.'"

What transpired next is the single most memorable moment of all my conversations with Maggy. The verbatim transcript reads, "It was a . . . Of course, thirty years after . . . all those wounded, I turned the page." The transcript doesn't capture the moment because those ellipses represent silence, and what I remember so distinctly is the way Maggy disappeared into the suspension of sound. According to the time stamps on the recording, what I remember as a *moment* lasted for one minute and forty seconds. What makes it memorable is that it's the only time I've ever witnessed just how close the events of October 24, 1993, remain for Maggy. She had always been clear about the way that day had shaped her life, but I had never watched as she disappeared back into the bishop's garden and into the chapel and on to the cemetery where Martin came to her rescue.

While disappearing into the silence of ellipses, Maggy started five sentences she didn't finish and finished only two without trailing off into silence. The verbatim transcript contains twenty ellipses, almost one for every five words. Counted as time, the ellipses represent more than a minute of silence, with the first ellipsis standing in for the longest stretch: "It was a . . ." Then thirteen seconds of silence during which I watched Maggy succumb to the gravitational pull of an invisible force, like an object orbiting a black hole. When she tried to speak again, she could muster only, "Of course, thirty years after . . ." Then four more seconds of silence.

When Maggy tried to speak for a third time, she modulated her voice into a tone I had never heard before, something close to the quiet timbre of a mother reading a story book to a child. "*But . . . some days . . .*" Then more than a minute of stuttering starts. "I ask God . . . I have a conflict with God. . . . Because I was raised in love with my mom. I . . . it's . . . it's why even Nkurunziza condemned me. Because I . . . I can't . . . I can't understand how a person can be so . . . bad . . . and kill. How can you kill the innocent? . . . Why this hatred? . . ."

Finally, the punch line. "Even now, I pray, when I pray, I say, 'God, you have a debt with me.'" Wanting to make sure I had heard her correctly, I asked, "'You have a debt with me,' that's what you say to God?" She replied: "Yes. Because I loved those people who became killers. How can they change so completely? How can that be? David, we are here, together today. And tomorrow, I see you with a weapon and you kill my friend?"

"This you can't understand," I said, as a declaration not a question. "Yes, this, and the motivation. Because even now I can't understand. Even now. It's why I will never keep silent. I will never keep silent because the atrocities I have seen move me—and the generosity of Martin and others who risked their lives for me. They didn't know me. Those who knew me, who were relatives, betrayed me. But those who didn't know me, they wanted to save me."

Even now is another of Maggy's favorite phrases. It's a counterpart to *It is like that*. The latter words often accompany a list of her inventions. They are her way of saying, "Good things have happened, and will continue to happen, because God is good, and the world is a wonderful place." It is like that.

Even now signals something else. "Even now, I am traumatized . . . Even now, we have war . . . Even now, I can't even think that Lydia and Lysette might die . . . Even now, I am in exile . . . Even now, I don't understand why God keeps abandoning us . . . Even now, God has a debt with me." It's noteworthy and revealing that Maggy's cancer does not make this list.

"Cancer is a wake-up call," Maggy says. "It reminds you that any day you can die." For most of us, that's a simple and unremarkable truth. But Maggy had received that reminder many times before. "They have been trying to kill me since 2007. Since then, they have tried to kill me. Even now, they use all methods to find and kill me." With death so close for so long, why was cancer different?

The answer rests in the contrast between two scenes in Maggy's storytelling. The first scene is one of her cancer. "I discovered the beauty of life," she says, followed immediately by "I was never alone." Cancer may have compelled Maggy into yet another argument with God, but it was not a sign that God had abandoned her. Quite the opposite. For Maggy, cancer became an occasion to experience divine love through the care of nurses and doctors and the constant presence of family and friends. The second scene is Maggy in the aftermath of the massacre in 1993. "And there I was . . . alone." The contrast between Maggy's account of her cancer and her description of what she experienced in 1993 exposes the full depth of her trauma.

~

The first time I saw Maggy after her cancer diagnosis and treatment was in Los Angeles in May 2024. She was there for the annual ceremony of the Aurora Prize, and she suggested that Nancy and I fly out to LA to see her. She hadn't changed since I was with her in April 2022, except she was a bit thinner, a bit tired, and subservient to a timer that beeped to let her know it was time for an insulin injection. Diabetes had become a byproduct of her immunotherapy, which she discovered in an emergency room in Brussels after having been rushed there in an ambulance.

Nancy and I spent two days with her before the Aurora ceremony, chatting over meals or gathered around a table in the lobby of the hotel. Over breakfast one morning Maggy was retelling the story of her cancer and updating us on her work in Rwanda. I asked her about the Mahama camp. She grabbed her phone to show pictures. What I saw was unrecognizable compared to the place I had visited in 2016. What had been haphazardly placed tents on a barren landscape was now row upon row of small brick houses, still tightly packed, but on tree-lined dirt streets with cultivated fields all around the edges. As we looked at the photographs, Maggy said, "We've made the impossible possible."

I noted the phrase. Maggy had said the same thing in some of the texts she'd sent during her cancer treatment. "We will make the impossible possible." Maybe she had been saying that for a long time, but later I did a word search of hundreds of pages of transcripts that go back fifteen years, and the phrase never appeared. It seems that in a life already undeterred by the seemingly impossible, cancer had caused Maggy to coin a new phrase, one that made explicit her long-standing worldview.

Regarding what possibility looked like in the Mahama camp, Maggy suggested we come see for ourselves. Two months later, Nancy and I arrived in Kigali on what happened to be Maggy's first day in a new home, a beautiful apartment in a building right next to Oasis of Peace and the offices of Maison Shalom. Just down the hill was Maggy's latest project: *École Sainte-Anne de Kigali*—ESAK for short—a nursery and primary school on its way to expanding into a high school and becoming certified as an International Baccalaureate (IB) school.

When I visited in 2016, Maggy had just started leasing the old hotel perched on one of Kigali's many hills, with a vision for turning it into the Oasis of Peace. She had talked then of a need for a nursery school for Burundian refugees, to help them stay connected to their culture in a foreign land, and of a community center that would do the same for adults. She had plans to develop the hotel's restaurant into both a source of income and a vocational training ground to prepare refugees for employment. Beyond that, she was dreaming of the Oasis of Peace in an almost literal way as a site where people from the conflict-burdened countries in the region of the African Great Lakes could come to find support for their efforts to create peace.

Most of that had now come to pass, but it had also been transformed. The lease turned into ownership. The nursery school became ESAK. Culinary training had moved to the Mahama camp because of a larger pool of talent. And Oasis of Peace had spun off a revenue-generating business with the same name: Oasis of Peace Ltd. In its business guise, Oasis of Peace uses its facilities to host conferences and orchestrate weddings and other celebratory events. It also harbors Elite Design, a firm that creates lines of clothing manufactured by refugees in the Mahama camp and then sold in a shop in Kigali.

What had changed the most in eight years, aside from robust program development, was a shift in Maison Shalom's organizational center of gravity. In 2016, Maison Shalom was working in the Mahama camp, but Maggy's energy and excitement were focused on the Oasis of Peace in Kigali. By 2024, the focus had shifted to ESAK and to the Mahama camp. These shifts came not as a change in mission but as organizational extensions of the Oasis of Peace—not unlike the way she kept building new centers in the early years of her work in Burundi: "You see, Casa della Pace, Oasis de Paix, Maison Shalom, they are all the same."

The one other significant change, an effect of Maggy's cancer that she had not anticipated, is that Richard Nijimbere was no longer the director of Maison Shalom. He had fled to Canada, and so had Emery Emerimana. Both had showed up at Maison Shalom as teenagers and been with Maggy for twenty-five years. Maggy had sent them to study in Russia together and then moved them up the ladder of leadership in Maison Shalom until they were wholly responsible for daily operations and had become anchors of the organization. That was true in Burundi and even more true in Rwanda when Maison Shalom had to start from scratch and reconfigure itself around the refugee crisis. Suddenly, they were gone.

Emery now works for the Belgian foundation from his home in Canada, and Maggy is hopeful that Richard will come back. Meanwhile, she understands. "To have lived through so much trauma. To be a refugee again, with a wife and kids. To have seen in Mahama people he knew in the camps in Tanzania. My cancer, the real possibility of my death, was just too much for Richard to stay in Rwanda as a refugee from Burundi facing an uncertain future."

~

The first thing Maggy wanted to show us when we arrived for our visit in July 2024 was the École Sainte-Anne de Kigali. It had opened just a year earlier and was publicly inaugurated in October 2023 with a celebration broadcast on TV and online. "You could follow it," Maggy says. "We were two hundred people from twenty-eight nationalities, and we had kids from Rwanda, Burundi, Congo, Cameroon, India . . ." She lets the list trail off. "And teachers from Kenya, from France, from Belgium, from Gabon." She added that she had heard through the grapevine that in the office of the president in Burundi they had stopped work and watched the event. "They were so angry to see it, to see that I continued to have success even in exile."

The impetus for building a school, Maggy explains, was her frustration with the educational options for refugees in Rwanda. Primary education for refugees is tuition-free in public and government-subsidized schools, but costs still add up. Students pay for their food, which schools are required to serve, and for uniforms, books, instructional materials, and examination fees. Secondary schools charge for these expenses as well as for tuition. "I have more than two thousand kids in school," Maggy says, "and it's very expensive. It hurt me to see what I was paying for education. I said, 'But why must I pay those schools when kids learn nothing? Why don't I build my own school? And then people can pay Maison Shalom.'"

To secure start-up funding, Maggy convinced Christian Solidarity International (CSI), a state-supported nonprofit in Luxembourg, to provide seed funding for construction. They were already working with Maison Shalom to help fund the placement of refugee children in Rwandan schools, so Maggy's pitch wasn't a stretch. Their support was modest, however, and only for a kindergarten. When Maggy broke ground in November 2021, she invited members of CSI to place the first stone. When they came back for the inauguration in October 2023 to find a full-fledged primary school designed to grow into a secondary school, they said, "Why don't we learn from Maggy?"

The comment was something of an inside joke. Years before in Burundi, CSI had provided forty thousand euros as seed funding for the modest start of Rema Hospital as a maternity center. When Maggy was done with that project, it had cost $10 million and included a 120-bed hospital, a nursing school, a medical school, and an expanded pediatric ward with forty incubators.

The school was headed in a similar direction. What started as a kindergarten had become a $1.8 million primary school; and when we toured the school in July 2024, Maggy was working to raise another $2 million to expand ESAK into a secondary school, a requirement for it to become certified as an IB school, which is an essential component of Maggy's business model. An IB certification will make ESAK competitive in an increasingly crowded Kigali educational market, attracting parents who can afford to pay fees that Maggy can use to subsidize the children of refugees.

Notably, however, IB certification is more than a business model. It also aligns with Maggy's fundamental views about what education should be. The International Baccalaureate Organization that certifies IB schools was founded as a nonprofit in Geneva in 1968, originally with the goal of establishing a rigorous, college-preparatory high school curriculum for the children of diplomats and others living outside their home countries. In time, however, the curricula expanded to include nursery school, kindergarten, primary school, and middle school—with a mission "to develop inquiring, knowledgeable, and caring young people who help to create a better and more peaceful world through intercultural understanding and respect."[10]

~

The IB model traces its roots back to the *École Internationale de Genève*—the world's first international school—and to the chaotic aftermath of World War II in Europe. In this respect, IB schools share something with two other institutions that have served as Maggy's sometimes antagonistic institutional interlocutors: SOS Children's Villages and UNHCR. Like these institutions, IB schools are the product of a devastating war that created tens of millions of refugees and millions of orphans in Europe and that destroyed the ability of entire nations to educate the next generation. I once heard Maggy remind well-intentioned people from the Global North who came to Africa preaching peace and troubling over its many violent and pro-tracted conflicts that, not so long ago, Americans and Euro-peans had all but leveled an entire continent—twice. It was a humbling moment for Maggy's audience.

The École Internationale de Genève was a product of World War I not World War II, but it was in the aftermath of the lat-ter that it became an early model for IB education, through the work of its long-time director, Marie-Thérèse Maurette, who led Geneva's international school from 1929 to 1949. In 1948, toward the end of her tenure, she wrote "Techniques d'education pour la paix," a twenty-three-page document sub-titled "Do They exist? Answer to a UNESCO Survey."[11]

Created six months after World War II had ended in Europe, UNESCO (United Nations Educational, Scientific, and Cul-tural Organization) was launched with the aim of preventing another world war by helping devastated countries rebuild their educational systems in ways that would create a culture of peace. The forty-four countries that came together for this purpose in November 1945 inscribed this aim in the opening lines of UNESCO's founding document: "The Governments of the States party to this Constitution on behalf of their peoples declare: That since wars begin in the minds of men, it is in the minds of men that the defences of peace must be constructed."[12]

Almost immediately after its creation, UNESCO started conducting field surveys of the state of education in Europe's war-torn countries while also surveying governments and educational experts. Marie-Thérèse's document on techniques of education for peace was a response to one of these surveys.[13] She wanted UNESCO to know that it might be possible to construct peace in the minds of children as a defense against war. She had been directing an experiment to do just that for almost twenty years: "Chance made a test attempt now almost 25 years old. In Geneva in 1924 some officials of the League of Nations, animated by faith in the institution they served, decided to create a school where their children would be raised in accordance with the new world that was believed to be built, a world of peace and understanding between nations."

In response to the survey, Marie-Thérèse sketched the four main components of Geneva's experiment with a pedagogy for peace: avoid creating feelings of superiority and national pride; create a vision of the whole world and the people who inhabit it; weaken, through a second language, the notion of foreigner; and create, in daily practice, a sense of social solidarity. The last item was especially important: "If it is a question of forming citizens of the world, who know their quality as citizens, we need an education that awakens the awareness of human solidarity."

The full description Marie-Thérèse used to summarize the second of these four educational techniques is telling: "To create in the minds of children, *very early,* a vision as exact as possible of the whole world and the living conditions of the men who inhabit it." As the IB curriculum developed over the years, "very early" came to be the ages three to twelve. Only in young children, Marie-Thérèse said, can you create "the attitude of 'human' feelings, surpassing the family, the social group, the nation. After all, proof has been made, abundantly, that one can create, through education, 'inhuman' attitudes. The bulk of the work must be done in childhood."

It's a cruel accident of circumstance—or, Maggy would say, strangely providential—that the inhuman events of 1993 would create the opportunity for Maggy to spend decades awakening the human in tens of thousands of Burundian children. Maggy first understood the necessity of constructing peace in the minds of children during the 1972 genocide, when her Tutsi teachers failed to acknowledge what was happening to their Hutu colleagues and students. "That's why I wanted to become a teacher, to denounce the lies that were parading as history." That's also why she stopped being a teacher after being fired for staging a play with her Hutu and Tutsi students. "I was young. I was twenty-four years old, and I couldn't continue to be a teacher when I couldn't teach the human values of compassion, integrity, solidarity."

Maggy may have left the classroom, but she didn't stop teaching, and she will tell you that one of her greatest accomplishments is what she left behind in Burundi in the form of Hutu–Tutsi solidarity through the construction of peace as a defense against ethnic violence in the minds of tens of thousands of orphans. She offers proof with another picture on her phone—this one of a coffin surrounded by people at a funeral in July 2016.

"You see they were together, Tutsi and Hutu. On this day, the government wanted to separate all the Hutu and the Tutsi. But they were all there together. Even the Hutu who are in power, who are part of the government right now, and who see me as the enemy. They were there." The funeral was for Bosco, the blind musician the government had killed two weeks before Maggy's sixtieth birthday.

∼

It would be hard to find a better summary of Maggy's life work than the founding declaration of UNESCO: "Since wars begin in the minds of men, it is in the minds of men that the defences of peace must be constructed." That work now continues in ESAK. Importantly, however, ESAK is more than an international school building toward IB certification; it is also an example of Maggy's adaptive response to a non-African institution that has been exported to Africa without a proper sense of the irony attached to its own origins in Europe's self-destruction.

The adaptive innovation that adds ESAK to the list of Maggy's inventions is the pairing of the IB curriculum with a pedagogy based upon the African conception of *ubuntu*. As a publicly proclaimed philosophy, *ubuntu* came on the scene in South Africa when the brutal segregation of apartheid was being dismantled in the early 1990s. Nelson Mandela sometimes used the term and once explained it by saying, "In Africa there is a concept known as *ubuntu*—a profound sense that we are human only through the humanity of others."[14] The person who really pushed the concept into the public sphere, however, was Desmond Tutu, the Anglican archbishop who led South Africa's post-apartheid Truth and Reconciliation Commission (TRC).

In a sermon in 1991, Tutu spoke of *ubuntu* to remind Black South Africans who they were: "It seems to me that we in the Black community have lost our sense of *ubuntu*—our humanness, caring, hospitality, our sense of connectedness, our sense that our humanity is bound up in your humanity. We are losing our self-respect, demonstrated, it seems to me, most graphically by the horrible extent of dumping and littering in our townships. Of course we live in squalor and slum ghettos. But we are not rubbish."[15]

More than a decade later, after the TRC process had run its course, Tutu invoked *ubuntu* in lectures in Europe when trying to explain why the TRC process didn't dismiss the perpetrators of horrific crimes as irredeemable monsters. "*Ubuntu* gives up on no one," he said. "We all, even the worst of us, remain children of God. We all retain the capacity to become saints."[16]

Maggy often says the same thing differently: "God has made us all princes and princesses." That's one of her favorite sayings. "We forget how amazing we are. We are princes and princesses. God gives us crowns." For Maggy, the fact that we are amazing follows from the Christian conception of *imago Dei*: human beings are made in the image of God. In a documentary about Maggy, the filmmakers captured a scene that puts this part of Maggy's worldview on clear display.[17]

The scene shows Maggy in Burundi before she fled into exile. She is in the welcoming area of the maternity center in Ruyigi. The space is full of mothers with infants waiting patiently for white-coated medical staff to call them forward one by one. It must have been a day for well-checks of some kind. She is instructing the staff to convey to the women the importance of hygiene. "You really have to inform them that they need to wash themselves. And you should also show them how to do it."

Then Maggy turns to the mothers. "When you ladies come to the hospital, it's not only to get medicine. You should leave this place clean and proper. You are queens. God has not done a bad job. Come, please, let me show you." Maggy then heads for the bathroom, followed by a line of women. In the small bathroom, the women crowd around Maggy, their babies strapped to their backs or in their arms. Before Maggy draws them into the sinks to show them how to wash, she points to the mirrors and says, "When you see yourself, you should say, 'I am created in his image.' And then look at your children and say, 'See the face of God.'"

Maggy's understanding that no one is rubbish, that anyone can be a saint, that we are all princes and princesses, rests in a Christian understanding of humanity; but it's also anchored in African conceptions of *ubuntu*, which not only hold up the invaluable nature of every individual but also underscore that no individual stands alone.

The depth of the concept is evident in the Bantu languages of sub-Saharan Africa. As an example, Bishop Tutu used the Xhosa language of South Africa: "In Xhosa, we say, '*Umntu ngumtu nagbantu.*'" As a translation, he offered, "A person is a person through other persons." A translation that has gained more traction is "I am because we are." Tutu also offered, "I am because I belong."[18] Close ties to the concept of *ubuntu* are common in many other Bantu languages, including Kirundi, Maggy's first language, where *amuntu* refers to a single human being and *abantu* to human beings in plural.

Tutu popularized *ubuntu* inside and outside South Africa in the 1990s, but it's an age-old African understanding of humanity. It's also been floating around as a word in English since at least 1860, when a missionary reporting on his work in South Africa wrote, "One man requires truth, love, righteousness in another, not falsehood, hatred, injustice; and this shows plainly what is *ubuntu*, the true, proper nature of a man."[19] Tutu explains: "In traditional African society, *ubuntu* was coveted more than anything else, more than wealth as measured in cattle and the extent of one's land. Those who had *ubuntu* were compassionate and gentle, they used their strength on behalf of the weak. If you lacked *ubuntu* in a sense you lacked an indispensable ingredient in being human."[20]

Maggy casts *ubuntu* in slightly different terms. She explained the concept one morning when we were together at the breakfast table, outside on the veranda of her fourth-floor apartment, with ESAK in full view just down the hill. "With *ubuntu* philosophy, to say that we want a world that is good, we must . . ." She breaks off the thought and backs up. "We are so lazy to think that we are simply part of humanity. We don't realize that if we are a member of humanity, then if somewhere people are suffering, it's part of our humanity that dies. Do we think about *that* when we wake up in the morning?" It's a rhetorical question, and she answers it by returning to where she started. "We are so lazy." Then she starts again:

> If somewhere, part of our humanity is suffering, it's an obligation for every human being to do something, because we are one human family. We can think, "Okay, for me, my children have enough to eat and are in good schools, and I'm happy." But those people who are suffering, they are part of our humanity. You can't be happy when you look on the TV and see that your humanity is suffering. When we die, the only thing they will ask us is, "What have you done for your brother and your sister?" And we should be able to say, "I stood up and I spoke out for all my humanity." This is *ubuntu* philosophy.

Having arrived where she started, she invokes the popular saying "I am because we are" but adds, "You can't exist when others are dying. Somewhere, you are dying too, because it's a part of your humanity. This has been my message for as long as I can remember, since I started speaking out and my family said, 'You make too much noise.'" Maggy then steps sideways, as she often does, trying to keep pace with her own mind, and starts talking about something that takes her back to the early years of trial in Burundi.

"You've seen the photo of me." It was not a question. Just inside the apartment on the coffee table in her living room, taking the place of the required coffee-table book, were two well-worn copies of *GEO* magazine. Both had articles about Maggy and Maison Shalom, written by the same reporter and accompanied by striking photographs. Not long after we had arrived in Maggy's apartment, she had picked up these magazines to show me the photographs, one of which I described earlier, when recounting the story of Caspar, the man who had killed one of her aunts. The first article, "A Saint in Hell," was from 1997; the second, a ten-year follow-up, was from 2008. The opening photograph of the first article, the same one that included a photograph of an emaciated Caspar, was of a young Maggy. With one arm, she was cradling an infant; with the other, she was securing a child of two or three to the opposite hip. She was smiling in a worn-out way.

"Look at me," Maggy says, referring to the photograph she knows I've seen. "Early in the morning, I look at this photo and I see how generosity changed my life. I had nothing and when I got something I gave it away and then people wanted to follow me and to transform the world. Because I stood up and made noise." Only later did I realize that Maggy had not sidestepped at all. In Kirundi, *ubuntu* is one of the words for generosity.

~

An explicit reference to *ubuntu* is new in Maggy's verbal and conceptual repertoire in English. Like her references to making the impossible possible, the term doesn't show up in word searches of transcripts going back to 2009. Implicitly, of course, *ubuntu* has been part of Maggy's life and work all along, as a deeply African conception of humanity inseparable from the languages that bear it.

If Maggy and I had been conversing in Kirundi all these years, we never would have been far from *ubuntu*, which is not to say that the term was missing in Maggy's English simply as a matter of translation. Maggy's explicit references to *ubuntu* are part of an effort to recover African conceptions of humanity for Africans. In this regard, she is following Mandela and Tutu. Speaking of ESAK's commitment to *ubuntu*, she says, "It's not about school for me. It's about dignity. We Africans, we have lost our soul."

ESAK's stated aim is to instill dignity, compassion, harmony, humility, and integrity in its students. The school ties this aim explicitly to *ubuntu*. "The concept of UBUNTU designates this aim to train men and women sharing a single humanity, engaged in their community to ensure the common good of each and all, ensuring respect for themselves, others and their environments."[21] Maggy has not limited her recovery of African conceptions of humanity to the children of ESAK. *Ubuntu* is also an anchor of Maison Shalom's work in Mahama, via the *Académie Ubuntu*—a mix of continuing education and vocational training for adult refugees in the camp.

The academy bills itself as a form of education "both innovative and ancient" that is "designed to strengthen the resilience of refugees and vulnerable populations." To explain the academy to prospective students in the Mahama camp, Maison Shalom invokes Desmond Tutu: "Ubuntu is the essence of being human. Ubuntu means that you cannot exist as a human being in isolation. Ubuntu is a reminder of our interdependence. You cannot be a human being alone; and when you are recognized as Ubuntu, you are recognized and celebrated for your generosity. Far too often we think of ourselves as just individuals, separate from each other, when in fact you are connected and what you do affects the whole world. When you do good, it radiates out and benefits all of humanity."[22]

It's easy to dismiss language like that as a string of platitudes until you visit the Mahama camp and witness Maison Shalom's programs firsthand, which Nancy and I did when we toured the camp with Maggy and a few other visitors as part of our July visit. We showed up in the dark because "on the way" Maggy wanted to take us to the wildlife park that sits just to the north of Mahama on the border between Rwanda and Tanzania. She confessed later that she sends visitors to the park but never goes herself. Our trip through the park had reminded her why. "I saw all those animals when I was young, still running around in Burundi. Now they exist on land protected for them while people living nearby are starving."

What the long drive through the park underscored for me is what the animals and refugees share: both have been pushed to the literal and figurative margins of a world that doesn't know what to do with them.

~

When we got to Mahama, we checked in to the small hotel refugees had built during the pandemic. It sits just outside the formal start of the camp. Once we had settled in, we ate dinner at the adjoining restaurant, also the work of refugees during the pandemic. Maggy let us know that the hotel and the restaurant were staffed entirely by refugees from the camp.

After breakfast in the morning, we started our tour on the edges of the camp, in the facilities of Maison Shalom, most of them dedicated to different forms of vocational training: the culinary arts, hairdressing and cosmetics, leather goods, and carpentry. Then we moved into the camp, where Maison Shalom has established a library and vocational training for sewing and computers. At the end of the tour, we drove to the edges of the camp and to the fields and agricultural facilities that are a leading edge of Maison Shalom's work with refugees in Mahama.

In every facility we entered, classes were in session and Maggy was greeted with singing and dancing, most memorably when we met the eighteen women that work for Maison Shalom as community health workers. Each of the women is assigned to one of the eighteen "villages" that define the camp's administrative organization. All are refugees living in the camp, and they are the link between Maison Shalom and residents. They track not only needs that emerge due to pregnancy and illness but also the education and well-being of children and vocational pathways for adults. More often than not, the students we met in the various vocational training centers were there because the community health workers had identified them as good prospects for one of Maison Shalom's centers.

The tour of Mahama reminded me of my 2009 visit to Ruyigi. The inventions were not exact replicas—no swimming pool or cinema or hospital or mechanics garage for child soldiers. But clearly they had emerged from the same imagination: a library, a beauty salon, a hotel and restaurant, a center for the culinary arts, a facility for clothing design and tailor training, a carpentry, a cobbler shop with cutting presses and lasting machines, a computer lab, an organic farm with chickens and cows and pigs, and a tennis court in the works. All of it was wrapped up in the same fundamental worldview that what people need most is hope for a future, paths to livelihood, and encouragement that they are amazing.

"I grew up in a family that taught me to be a builder of hope, of new community, of humanity. We must shine in this life," Maggy says. "It's the only mission we have on Earth. When God created us, he said, 'Go and make this Earth into paradise.' It's not so difficult. We just don't realize that we have an exceptional, amazing vocation. When I am trying to transform Mahama, I am full of hope because in Mahama there are twenty-nine thousand young people. You have seen them. They are refugees like me. We fled together, and I know that when we return, they will do amazing things."

A single scene sticks with me from our visit to Mahama. Others surround it like a musical accompaniment—scenes of Maggy speaking to whole rooms of refugees as timid smiles break through impassive faces, scenes of the same rooms greeting Maggy with song and dance. But one scene stands out. We were in the vocational training center dedicated to carpentry. It was our last stop before hopping in the vehicles and driving into the camp. Maggy let us know that refugees working in this center had made all the furniture in the restaurant and hotel and in Maison Shalom's other facilities. I was impressed by the industrial quality of the equipment, closer to what you would find in a furniture manufacturing plant than in a carpenter's garage. As we entered, the instructor and ten students set aside their various projects to greet us.

Nine of the students were young men; one was a young woman. She withdrew behind the men, but Maggy called her forward and then launched into a speech in Kirundi, a version of the pep talk she had given when we visited the other centers, or so it seemed to me. At one point, however, I noticed the reaction was different: shifting feet, more frequent smiles, glances at one another. I asked for translation from the man standing next to me, one of the many Burundians from the diaspora that Maggy has pulled into her orbit.

"She is telling them that she knows carpentry is not glamourous, but that it's a good skill to have, that they will get jobs and make money, and that it will give them something to do. She wants them to know that this is important, because some men will come and offer to train them for a different kind of job. They will teach them to kill. Maggy is saying that because of what they are learning here, they will be able to turn those men away."

I had heard this refrain from Maggy before, many times. Refugees turn into rebels. It's an African story, one that Maggy is trying to change. I had heard it but never witnessed how close to the surface that possibility is in the lives of refugees, nor the way the work of Maison Shalom is designed to counter its likelihood. I also had never heard Maggy confess, as she did later, that she understands the temptation to take up arms and return to Burundi to unseat a government that continues to torture and kill its own people. It's a temptation she has had to combat in her own soul. "Because of what's happening to my people in Burundi, I've imagined returning with weapons, but then I would belong to the killers." What I saw as I watched Maggy's speech animate those ten carpenters-to-be—ten out of twenty-nine thousand—was the seeding of an alternative to violence. "It's a small drop in this big ocean," Maggy said later, "but the value of this drop . . ." She didn't finish the sentence, but I understood: dignity, compassion, harmony, humility, integrity. The future depends on the recovery of *ubuntu*.

~

"So your dream is to make Mahama like Ruyigi?" Someone in our group asked Maggy the question. She replied, "Better, because I have learned from being here in Rwanda, where everything was destroyed in 1994." In that answer, I heard a clue to something I'd been unable to account for: Mahama *was* like Ruyigi, but without sites like the mass grave and the burned-out village.

In Ruyigi, sites of death and destruction had served as sources for Maggy's life-giving imagination, but Maggy's work in Rwanda did not seem to be a response to similar sites. The Mahama camp was out of the way, but it didn't sit on the ruins of a village or on the former site of an artillery battery. Exile had changed the way Maggy told her story, and for a time I thought that perhaps its impact on Maggy had overtaken the trauma of 1993 and untethered her imagination from sites of violence. But then Maggy reminded me that in Rwanda in 1994, "Everything was destroyed."

All of Rwanda is effectively a mass grave, a reality underscored in more than two hundred genocide memorials, with the preferred design featuring a prominent display of skeletal remains. One such memorial is in Nyarubuye. Over three days in April 1994 more than fifty thousand people were murdered in and around the town. Twenty thousand of those murders occurred inside the Catholic church. None of the most horrific acts that defined the brutality of the genocide were left uncommitted in Nyarubuye: rape, the disemboweling of pregnant women, the killing of small children by smashing their heads against a wall. The mass grave at the Nyarubuye memorial contains the remains of fifty-one thousand people.[23] Mahama is ten miles away.[24]

Maggy is not a fan of Rwanda's memorials. As she sees them, their graphic depiction of the violence leveled against the Tutsi paired with a "never again" narrative is not an invitation to reconciliation. "Imagine being a Hutu in Rwanda." Her view has deep roots, apparent in her own memorial for the seventy-two victims of the massacre. The Prayer of St. Francis on the memorial at the mass grave in Ruyigi is an invitation to peace, not a reminder of the crime. Originally, Maggy had listed the names of the victims on the memorial, but they kept disappearing, presumably because the killers, who were still part of the community, saw the names as a condemnation they were unwilling to accept. Because the memorial was becoming a site of conflict, Maggy replaced the names of the dead with the Prayer of St. Francis.

Maggy's view of memorializing genocide is also apparent in how she remembers the anniversary of October 24, 1993. That's when she celebrates her successes. The inauguration of ESAK took place on October 24, and so have all the celebratory anniversaries of Maison Shalom. "People tell me that I must not celebrate the twenty-fourth of October. That we should dress in black and be quiet because on that day they killed people. But I say, 'We are not celebrating death but victory. They died, but we are here, building hospitals and schools.' This is my message."

Maggy's imagination hasn't changed. She's still following the same logic she did in Burundi. Where hatred or death have left a wasteland, she's creating life. The scale of the blueprint is simply larger. It's not an exaggeration to say that everything was destroyed in Rwanda in 1994, nor that what the country has become since rests, all too literally, on the mass graves of a million people slaughtered in a hundred days. What Maggy has learned from Rwanda is the scope of possibility; it's greater than she had imagined when she was working to turn Ruyigi into paradise.

Trying to track Maggy's imagination, I asked her if I was right to have noticed what seemed to be a shift in focus from the Oasis of Peace as a center for refugees in Kigali in 2016 to all the activity I witnessed in the Mahama camp in 2024. "Yes. My dream is to transform Mahama because the region is the future for the East African community. Mahama is in Rwanda; across the river is Tanzania; and you can reach Burundi in thirty minutes. The river is fertile. More than seventy thousand people live there. Imagine. You could build an economy that transforms the region: crops to feed Tanzania, Burundi, and Rwanda; bakeries for bread; milk and cheese; and manufacturing—fabrics and furniture. With vision, we can make many industries. We can transform this suffering into opportunity because we have young people with talent."

Here was Maggy's imagination playing out at scale: "It's my dream of the Oasis of Peace. In countries where there has been so much conflict, instead of thinking of fighting, people would have something to do. We can create a chain of transformation. Why don't we make a hub here so the young will not risk their lives in the Mediterranean Sea? Africa is blessed. Africa is the future of the world. What I can't understand is why people are so lazy, sitting there waiting and talking."

Maggy is not waiting, and to be fair, neither is Rwanda. Indeed, the traction Maggy and Maison Shalom have gained in the Mahama camp is the result of a remarkable alignment between Maggy's vision and the goals of the Rwandan government. A well-organized, stable country surrounded by political instability on three sides, Rwanda is a magnet for refugees. Its response to this reality is novel and is perhaps not unrelated to the fact that President Paul Kagame grew up as a refugee in neighboring Uganda after his parents fled there in 1959 to escape the violence leveled against the Tutsi during the Hutu revolution. When they fled, he was two years old. When he returned in 1990 as the commander of the Rwandan Patriotic Front, he was thirty-five.

Instead of shunning refugees, Rwanda works to integrate them as quickly as possible, turning necessity into opportunity. As soon as they arrive, refugees receive identity cards that make them eligible to work and to start businesses, with access to financial services. Rwanda doesn't have enough jobs for its 135,000 refugees, but integration is the goal.

As of July 2024, roughly 10 percent of the refugees in the Mahama camp have been economically integrated into Rwandan society. The camp manager, who works for Rwanda's Ministry of Emergency Management, told us on our tour of Mahama that the goal is to double that number over the next three years, with a final aim of 60 percent integration. Were those numbers to represent the end of the Mahama camp at some point in the future, roughly forty thousand Burundians would have become Rwandans, and the remaining thirty thousand would have moved on or returned to Burundi.

Unsurprisingly, given these goals, Maison Shalom's educational and vocational programs in Mahama are a boon to the Rwandan government, but Maggy's vision represents a bit of a departure from the goals of both Rwanda and UNHCR. "It's not a camp," she says. "It's a city. The refugees can go to town, Kigali or any other, and work, or even to Uganda or some other country. They can leave for work and come back. They can cross the border into Tanzania and do business. There's a market. They can shop. Maison Shalom gives loans to women, and they create their own businesses. There are two health centers and a school, and farms nearby." As Maggy sees it, the word "camp" suggests an impermanence that no longer applies to Mahama.

~

Maggy has suggested to both Rwanda and UNHCR that they rename the camp Mahama City. She made the case to Filippo Grandi, the United Nations High Commissioner for Refugees, on a trip to Geneva. The United Nations created the position of high commissioner and the accompanying agency in 1950 to address the plight of the forty to fifty million refugees in Europe at the end of World War II. Over time, its mandate expanded. Its current charge is "to lead and coordinate international action for the worldwide protection of refugees and the resolution of refugee problems."

Maggy recounts Grandi's response to her suggestion of a name change for the Mahama refugee camp. "He laughed, 'You want me to lose my job?' I said, 'Yes, I dream of no refugees, anywhere in the world. Then you would lose your job.'" Maggy continues, "He's a good guy, an Italian, and when I said that, he laughed some more. Then I told him he was a hypocrite because UNHCR gives us travel documents that don't work well for travel. No one recognizes them. I said that UNHCR should advocate for an immigration line called 'UN Convention.' As it is, when we arrive in airports, we have nowhere to go."

Immigration services at airports, Maggy explains, have lines for "Passports" and "Visas" but not for the official document refugees carry: a passport-like document stamped on the front with the UNHCR emblem and the words "Travel Document," beneath which it says in parentheses, "Convention of 28 July 1951." The reference is to Article 28 of the Convention Relating to the Status of Refugees: "States shall issue to refugees lawfully staying in their territory travel documents for the purpose of travel outside their territory; they shall in particular give sympathetic consideration to the issue of such a travel document to refugees in their territory who are unable to obtain a travel document from the country of their lawful residence."

Maggy doesn't make the connection explicit, but there is a moral to the story of her exchange with Filippo Grandi about Mahama City and UNHCR travel documents. For years, her vision was of Burundi as a country without orphans. The intent was not simply to care for orphans but to create a world in which orphans don't exist. Maggy's vision now follows the same logic. What Maison Shalom started as a series of programs to care for refugees in Rwanda has become Maggy's vision of a world without them. "We have one passport that God has given us; we are citizens of the world. We must share things—there is enough for everybody, and we can be happy without war."

I was with Maggy in the office of the camp manager when she made her case to him. "This is the dream I want you to work with me to announce, the word to spread, 'Welcome to Mahama City. We refuse to be refugees. We want to be citizens of the world.'" He didn't respond directly to the comment but praised Maggy and Maison Shalom for what they were doing in the camp. It was clear that Maggy was baiting him, and he knew it. If the camp truly became a city, he wouldn't have a job. For the time being, his job is safe. He and Maggy both know that a name change now would be aspirational, not descriptive.

When Maggy recounts her dream of turning the border lands of Rwanda, Tanzania, and Burundi into a hub of economic activity that would become the engine of East Africa, she is casting a vision for the future of Mahama City. It's a vision with a surprising feature. "We won't even need to return to Burundi." Nearly a decade of exile paired with seven months of cancer treatment are bound up in that comment and what it gestures toward.

"During the months I was outside Rwanda in hospital, I realized that my vocation is not to stay in this Great Lakes region. I must also give testimonial all over the world. Three American universities have given me honorary degrees. I have received the Aurora Prize for Awakening Humanity, and the Opus

Prize. I had time in hospital, you see. During seven months, praying, because I need . . . I rented a room in the convent . . ." Maggy didn't finish the sentence, but the meaning was clear. Whatever would come after exile would no longer simply be a return to Burundi.

~

When I think of what Maggy's vision has become, Mohsin Hamid's novel *Exit West* jumps to mind. *Exit West* is a love story wrapped in a thought experiment about a world without refugees.[25] I read the novel not long after it came out in 2017, a few months before Maggy's impromptu trip to visit me in Durham, which is when I first noticed the impact exile was having on her worldview. The novel came to mind then, and it comes to mind now because it helps us imagine the world Maggy envisions.

The novel opens in an unnamed city at some point in the future, but not a time overly distant from the present. Though unnamed, the city could be Lahore, Pakistan, the city of Hamid's birth. The story begins with the words, "In a city swollen by refugees . . ." At the start of the novel, the city is "teetering at the edge of the abyss" but "not yet openly at war." Soon, however, battles between rebel militias and government forces "raged without meaningful interruption" and war "revealed itself to be an intimate experience."

In the early pages, Hamid drops only a few hints of his thought experiment, which involves imagining a world in which everyday doors—in modest apartments, in alleyways, in mansions—turn into portals to other places in the world. In one early scene, we read of a woman "far away in Australia" and of the doorway to her bedroom closet, "a rectangle of complete darkness," out of which a dark-skinned man emerged. Later we encounter a similar scene, this time in an alley outside a bar in Tokyo when two Filipina girls emerged from "a disused door to the rear of the bar, a door that was always kept locked."

None of these scenes make sense until a third of the way through the novel, when the narrator says, "Rumors had begun to circulate that the doors could take you elsewhere, often to places far away, well removed from this deathtrap of a country. Some people claimed to know people who knew people who had been through the doors. A normal door, they said, could become a special door, and it could happen without warning, to any door at all." Soon rumors became reality and "even the most reputable international broadcasters had acknowledged the doors existed, and indeed were being discussed by world leaders as a major global crisis."

The turning point in Hamid's thought experiment comes midway through the novel when doors start opening all over Britain, with an unusually high number in London mansions, leading to violent clashes between migrants and "nativist" mobs. Elsewhere around the world, the news "was full of war and migrants and nativists, and was full of fracturing too, of regions pulling away from nations, and cities pulling away from hinterlands, and it seemed that as everyone was coming together everyone was also moving apart. Without borders nations seemed to be becoming somewhat illusory, and people were questioning the role they had to play."

In Britain, nativists were "advocating wholesale slaughter," which is how things went for a while. Then "something seemed to have happened, for there was a pause, and the natives and their forces stepped back from the brink." No one knew why. "Perhaps they decided they did not have it in them to do what would have needed to be done, to corral and bloody and where necessary slaughter the migrants. Irrespective of the reason, decency on this occasion won out, and bravery, for courage is demanded not to attack when afraid."

As the people of London were coming to terms with stepping back from the brink, "the whole planet was on the move. All over the world people were slipping away from where they had been, from fertile plains cracking with dryness, from seaside villages gasping beneath tidal surges, from overcrowded cities and murderous battlefields." In London, they decided to build "a ring of new cities that would be able to accommodate more people again than London itself. This development was called the London Halo, one of innumerable human halos and satellites and constellations springing up in the country and in the world."

Hamid's thought experiment doesn't end in paradise. "Adjustment to this new world was difficult. Disruptions were enormous, and conflict did not vanish overnight, it persisted and simmered, but reports of its persistence and simmering seemed less than apocalyptic. The apocalypse appeared to have arrived and it was not apocalyptic and people found ways to be and people to be with, and plausible desirable futures began to emerge, unimaginable previously, but not unimaginable now."

In an interview, Mohsin Hamid was asked about the doors in *Exit West*: "The doors," he said, "were at the very center of the idea for this book. What I'm trying to explore is how everyone is a migrant." When asked about the anger toward migrants that "seems to be afoot in the world," Hamid responded, "I think we're failing in our imaginations."

~

Our failures are often failures of imagination, and the world we live in is the cumulative result. "For as long as I can remember," Maggy says, "I have tried to imagine the world differently." The difference between Maggy and most of the rest of us is that her imagination has found real purchase. A village leveled in a fit of genocidal violence became a hospital. An artillery battery became a maternity ward. A mass grave became a swimming pool. A refugee camp became a city. *Là où est abondit la haine ou la mort je voulais faire vivre la vie,* Maggy says in French: "Where hatred or death left a wasteland, I wanted to create life." When Maggy imagines a world without refugees, she's not being romantic. She sees a plausible desirable future that may be unimaginable to us, but it's not unimaginable to her.

One of Maggy's favorite songs is John Lennon's "Imagine." She ignores the lines "Imagine there's no heaven / And no religion, too." Laughing, she says, "I'm sure he's in heaven, and when I meet him there, I'll point out his mistake." She often holds up other verses in the song as a summary of her life and of the world as she envisions it: "Imagine there's no countries / Nothing to kill or die for / Imagine all the people / Sharing all the world / You may say I'm a dreamer / But I'm not the only one / I hope someday you'll join us / And the world will live as one."

The doors in *Exit West* are aids for us to imagine the world as Maggy imagines it. The novel is a good fit for this exercise because Maggy's imagination was born out of the same worldly material that Hamid used to create his doors: murderous battlefields, war as an intimate experience, the deathtrap of a country, a city full of refugees, nations becoming somewhat illusory. It's from that material in her own life that Maggy has imagined a world without refugees. As in the novel, she knows that the path to the world she imagines is one of jarring change and enormous disruption, but it won't be apocalyptic. A plausible desirable future really will materialize. Decency will prevail, and courage, as those poised for violence pull back from the brink. Life will go on. People will find new ways to be.

~

The trip Nancy and I took to Rwanda in July 2024 was a whirlwind. The metaphor is apt. We stayed with Maggy for ten days, ungrounded from our own lives and pulled into the vortex of hers. Phone calls, text messages, visitors, travel, more phone calls and texts and visitors. Maggy was never alone, and conversations in one medium or another were constant. I kept trying to find time to whisk Maggy away for a final interview, but anything impromptu was proving impossible, so we set a time toward the end of the visit, one that would be free of distraction and interruption and allow a focus on my lingering questions.

Our conversation took place in a sitting room in her apartment, where she goes to watch the news. My first question on a long list concerned money. People often ask how Maggy has been able to fund all her remarkable work. I've never had a good answer. Richard, then the director of Maison Shalom, once told me that between 1994 and 2015, Maison Shalom raised $55 million for its inventions in Burundi. Almost ten years of work in Rwanda has certainly run up that tab. I've known bits and pieces of Maison Shalom's funding but never grasped the details. The night before Maggy and I met for a closing conversation, however, I witnessed something that struck me as essential to Maggy's funding model.

A visitor had come to see Maggy. He was from Ethiopia, the director of an NGO working in Mahama. He and Maggy were seated outside on the veranda of Maggy's apartment. It was another beautiful evening with a panoramic view of the lights of Kigali. I joined them and listened in. Maggy was describing a new project she wanted to start in the camp. What struck me about the scene was that she appeared to be brokering a deal. When we sat down for our closing conversation, I asked her about the meeting.

She said the government and other NGOs were resisting her new project. Her visitor and his staff were new to Mahama and not yet settled into the politics of aid in the camp, so she saw an opportunity. She wanted to get all the big players on board but needed help building a coalition. She was maneuvering to create an ally. The explanation led her to talk about how she had operated in Burundi. "When I sold six hundred tons of rice to

the World Food Programme, we had a memorandum of understanding. We also signed an MOU with UNHCR to take care
of Congolese refugees, and with UNICEF we had had an agreement to care for kids in conflicts with the law. We had had an
agreement with WHO for the healthcare we provided in Rema
Hospital. By 2015, we had agreements with every UN agency."

I asked, "Now you're doing something similar in the camp?"
Maggy replied, "Yes, because love makes us inventors. When
you love, you will find the way to give people dignity." For
Maggy, the ways have been many. She has become adept at brokering partnerships with UN agencies and with governments,
foundations, and individual donors. The funding of Rema Hospital is a good example. I knew that the $1 million Opus Prize
had been instrumental in building the hospital, but I didn't
know anything about how she raised the remaining $9 mil-
lion. Maggy rattled off a list. "I started with forty thousand
euros from CSI in Luxembourg. Then I got funds from a family foundation in Switzerland. And from my friend Véronique,
through her family foundation in Luxembourg. And from the
queen too, for the maternity ward. And from the French government, for the lab, and Germany—banks in Germany. And
in France, also a businessman, he paid for an expanded neonatal unit and maternity ward. And a bank in Italy, through a
hospital in Milano. And UNICEF, in Germany . . ."

The list caused Maggy to jump to the early years of Maison
Shalom. "The Swiss government, they sent me twenty-two tons
of powdered milk, in shipping containers, for the babies. And
the minister of defense in Germany, he sent a plane with mat-
tresses. We were sleeping on cardboard and beds made with
grass. Imagine, the very first materials I received were mat-
tresses from the minister of defense in Germany. And journal-
ists, we got a lot of money from the *GEO* article in 1997. Even
Japan, the Japanese government sent me money." Once again,
"It is like that" is rhythmically implied.

~

After the question about funding, my list was long. Some questions were matters of clarification about stories I had heard before. Who had untied her from the chair in 1993? When did she turn the curtains into clothes? When she received the text from the men sent to kill her, what exactly had she done next? Other questions were new, having emerged from conversations or encounters during the previous days. I knew of Bosco but had never really tracked his story—could she retell it? The 1997 *GEO* article on her coffee table said that her mother was an orphan. Could she say more?

As always, Maggy took each question in turn, and her answers always gave me more than I asked for. The only interruption came when her phone rang. She glanced at the phone but didn't answer. "I know what they want, but I will . . . I am trying . . ." The call was from a young man in prison in Burundi. Such calls had come in frequently during our stay with Maggy. "It's very hard for me, sometimes. Because they tortured them, and I am obliged, imagine, to pay the criminals to free the young men. And this is . . . it's not in my philosophy, but when you think that it's a young man, only twenty-nine years old, and he did nothing, he committed no crime, and they oblige you to pay $10,000."

Maggy paused and gestured around her apartment. "Always somewhere the cross, somewhere a rosary. And I pray, 'Must I pay this criminal and save?' We have thirteen thousand young people in jail in Burundi, but in the situation where they are, it's not a prison. They are there to die. And to save these people, I have to pay, to give them . . ." Maggy pauses. "To rebuild my motherland." She paused again; then, more to herself than to me, "Why?"

Her answer was heartbreaking. "Because I was so happy

when I was young. We always had food—vegetables and fruit. Now people are suffering, even from hunger. They are being tortured and killed. This morning, they sent pictures. And I said, 'My God. What? How? How can it be that in forty years this beautiful country has become a hell?' I was thinking about Jesus crying for Jerusalem."

The reference is to a scene in Luke's Gospel: "As he came near and saw the city, he wept over it, saying, 'If you, even you, had only recognized on this day the things that make for peace! But now they are hidden from your eyes'" (Luke 19:41–42).

~

The unanswered phone call was a brief interruption in a conversation that was moving toward a natural end as my questions dwindled. When I was down to my last one, I let Maggy know. "I have one final question," I said. "I'm not sure how to phrase it, so I'll ask it in two or three different ways, starting with, 'What are your hopes for the future?'"

> My hope has its roots in my faith. What I am sure of, the conviction I have, is that love will win. I am never anxious about what will happen. For me it's not a problem. Because I know that before he died, Jesus promised, "Don't be afraid. I am with you until the end of the world." It's not my job to save the world. I know that I am in his hands. We, the world, are in the hands of the creator. I am sure that evil will never take the last word. Never. Jesus is there, and he said to us, "Don't be afraid." My hope is on the cross. He won on the cross. He won. He didn't fail. Our human eyes think, "Oh, he died." He didn't die. He returned.

Maggy laughed. "This is my hope, because of my faith. 'Who will be against us?' Who? You see, *Qui nous séparera de l'amour de Dieu?*"

In both English and French, Maggy was quoting from Saint Paul's letter to the Romans: "We know that all things work together for good for those who love God, who are called according to his purpose. What then are we to say about these things? *If God is for us, who is against us? Who will separate us from the love of Christ?*" (Romans 8:28–33).

Maggy added a question. "Who will make us afraid?" Maybe here, too, she was thinking of Saint Paul. "The Lord said to Paul in a vision, 'Do not be afraid, but speak and do not be silent, for I am with you, and no one will lay a hand on you to harm you, for there are many in this city who are my people" (Acts 18:9–10). That passage certainly aligns with Maggy's life. "We are the winner always," she said. "Jesus won. And it's why you see me on Sunday, putting on my best clothes to celebrate the victory of love over death, of life over death. Yes. This is my hope."

I'm not sure how I expected Maggy to answer my question, nor, as I had indicated to her, even exactly what my question was, but I think I was expecting something more concrete, like, "My hope is that my exile will end and that I will return to Burundi." Regrouping, I said, "Okay, let me ask a similar question, with a slightly different word. What's your dream?"

Without the slightest pause, Maggy answered, "I dream of transforming the world into paradise. People think I am fighting to return to my country, but I am fighting for an end to stupidity. Some people are dying because they eat too much. Others die because they have nothing. Second and third houses sit empty while people are out on the street. I dream of an end to all stupidity. I dream of going to the UN in New York and saying to all the representatives, 'Stop being stupid.' This is my dream."

It was my turn to laugh, and then Maggy explained her view of the world order. UN conferences, she said, are fashion shows, and the world order is a lab populated by politicians whose only purpose is to stay in power and defend the status quo. "All those people who kill, they kill out of ignorance or indifference. It's not hatred that kills. The real criminals are not the killers but the politicians in office who plan and manipulate, who set things up this way. They are there in their lab. They will never ... There is no justice. I don't want ..." What she was aiming for went unfinished. Then she said, "I will not see all the change I want; it will take time. I will be in heaven, dancing. When I die, Saint Peter will ask me, 'Maggy, what have you done?' and I will say, 'I tried.'" She laughed as she described the scene.

Epilogue

As I noted in the preface, this book took me a long time to write. Along the way, there were many distractions, unanticipated events, and ongoing conversations with Maggy. I didn't know I was writing a book until, somehow, I was. But there was also the deeper challenge of writing about Maggy in a way that was accurate in both a narrow sense—when and where this or that happened—and a more profound sense, that is, in a way that conveys the truth of Maggy's life.

Once when I expressed concern to Maggy about the accuracy of my storytelling, she said, "There are four accounts of Jesus's life, and they are all true." On another occasion, I told her that when I had finished telling her story I would have what I had written translated into French and give it to her to read to make sure I had gotten things right. She said, "Oh, that won't be necessary. If you make it clear that God is good, then what you have written will be right."

That might sound like she was giving me a lot of leeway and that I was getting off the hook, but in fact she had given me an almost insurmountable challenge, of the sort Thomas Keneally described when writing about his efforts to tell the story of Oskar Schindler in *Schindler's List:* "When you chronicle the predictable and measurable success evil generally achieves—it is easy to be wise, wry, piercing, to avoid bathos. It is easy to show the inevitability by which evil acquires what you could call the *real estate* of the story, even though good might finish up with a few imponderables like dignity and self-knowledge. But it is a risky enterprise to have to write of virtue."[1]

Keneally insisted that his story about Schindler escaped imponderables: "This is the story of the pragmatic triumph of good over evil, a triumph in eminently measurable, statistical, unsubtle terms." Keneally put it that way because Schindler's great feat was to save more than 1,200 Jews from almost certain death in concentration camps by keeping them employed in his factories through bribery and deceit. As Keneally saw it, those 1,200 lives were a measurable victory. Probably he was wrong, or at least it is not clear to me that there are any statistical victories against evil. As the German philosopher T. W. Adorno once pointed out, statistics always tip in the other direction: "an overwhelming number of killed with a minimal number of rescued."[2] That fact leaves the challenge Keneally identified on the table. How do you write about the triumph of good over evil, of hope over despair, when victory looks like defeat?

Without doubt, what looks like defeat is part of Maggy's story. Rema Hospital, Maggy's crowning achievement in Burundi, now sits empty, all its equipment stolen or vandalized. The government even sold the ambulance. "How can you sell an ambulance?" Maggy asks. "The medical school they destroyed. They took the windows, the doors, they destroyed all the equipment. They destroyed everything: the library, the swimming pool. They took the seats out of the cinema and transformed it into a bar. They sold my clothes publicly, the clothes of a 'criminal.' And my car, and my furniture. The secretary general of the CNDD-FDD, the ruling political party, now lives in my house, and the militia moved into my chapel."

~

What's left but imponderables? Maggy's story is full of them. That's what makes her story compelling, and what compelled me to tell it. At the start of this book, when I quoted the Prayer of St. Francis, I said that I had come to understand that this was Maggy's prayer and that in Maggy the Lord had answered it. I also said I was making that assessment as someone not convinced that there is a Lord who answers prayers. Then I added the caveat, "Nonetheless, Maggy Barankitse is convincing."

Now I can be more specific, thanks to Kavin Rowe, my colleague at Duke. A New Testament scholar, Kavin sometimes finds himself arguing with other New Testament scholars concerning the question, "Why study the New Testament?" The answer, he suggests, is simple and one rarely entertained in New Testament scholarship: "We should study the New Testament because it might tell the truth about God."[3] What's not simple, Kavin says, is how to explain what that means, because of what we take truth to be.

Most often, we think of truth as the verifiable correspondence between what we say about the world and the world itself as an empirical entity. Kavin suggests, however, that "the New Testament does not primarily ask its readers to evaluate the correspondence of its assertions with the exterior world; its emphasis is rather on trusting the truth enough to live by it, a kind of hanging of your existence on the truth by the style of life you adopt and exhibit."

When I say that Maggy is convincing, that her life has collapsed into the biblical narrative, that in some sense she has become a biblical character, I mean it in this way. Maggy hangs her entire existence on the biblical narrative as it is condensed into a single truth: "God so loved the world that he gave his only Son" (John 3:16).

Maggy once confirmed for me that this is the truth she trusts with her life. I was trying to make sense of Maggy theologically—in particular, how she has thought about her own trauma. To set up the conversation, I asked her how she understood the progression of the passion narrative, from the crucifixion and burial on Friday, to the sealing of the tomb on Saturday, to the empty tomb and resurrection on Sunday. I set things up this way because I had been reading about trauma, theologically considered, and had encountered this sentence in Shelly Rambo's book *Spirit and Trauma*: "The terrible memory of suffering cannot be addressed by gazing at the cross. Instead, the gaze is from the middle. The gaze is a gaze of the cross as it is handed over to those who remain."[4]

When I read that sentence, I thought immediately of Maggy as the one who remained after being handed the cross seventy-two times. Here's how Rambo explains the *middle*: "Trauma is not solely located in the actual event, but instead encompasses the return of that event. For those who survive trauma, the experience of trauma can be likened to a death, but the reality is that death has not ended; instead, it persists. The structure of trauma introduces what I refer to as 'the middle,' the figurative site in which death is no longer bounded. Instead, the middle speaks to the perplexing space of survival."

In the context of the passion narrative as it is taken up into Christian worship during the week of Easter, this middle space is Holy Saturday, a time between death and resurrection. Wondering if Maggy's self-understanding would confirm Rambo's description of a middle space between cross and resurrection, despair and hope, I asked Maggy how she thought of her life in the context of the passion narrative as embodied in Easter worship. What she said was more complicated than I expected.

She acknowledged that Saturday is important because it is a time of mourning. "On Saturday, I take time to mourn what happened at the cross, to recognize that even Jesus was in a tomb. This is the silence that prepares the way for the wonder of the resurrection." I asked, "So does that make Saturday the most powerful day, or is it Sunday?" Maggy answered, "Neither. For me, it's Friday, when love is hung on a tree. Imagine. Imagine how wonderful it is for the love of God to accept humiliation on the cross. That's the most powerful."

No doubt, the cross is a powerful testament to life in a world of suffering, but I've never known what to do with the words "God so loved the world that he gave his only Son," especially when encountered on billboards along the highway, where the message is often broadcast simply as John 3:16, as if chapter and verse alone are sufficient to secure assent to this central tenet of Christianity.

Kavin has helped me see these words differently: "Sentences such as 'God so loved the world' are not so much to be met with an 'I agree with or assent to that' as they are with a pattern of life that shows what its truth means. The entire Gospel of John assumes that 'God so loved the world' is a way of life." When I say that Maggy is convincing, this is the kind of truth I have in mind. The life she lives defines the truth she trusts.

~

What Maggy built in Burundi may lie in ruins, but she is undeterred. Even more, she has bigger dreams. "I dream of transforming the world into paradise." She anchors that dream in Mahama City: a hub for Africa, and for the future of the world. The idea is perhaps not as crazy as it sounds. José María Arizmendiarrieta, a Catholic priest in Spain, had a similar dream for the region of Mondragón in 1941, after the region had been wracked by the Spanish Civil War. The Mondragón Corporation, a worker-owned cooperative, now employs eighty thousand people and generates billions of dollars in annual revenue. Mondragón has not changed the world, but it has changed a region.[5]

Even Maggy's more ambitious dream of Mahama City as a catalyst for transforming the world into paradise has an anchor in reality. The world rests on such urban hubs, and new ones are cropping up in Africa and elsewhere all the time, designed from scratch to be economic and social engines for the future.[6]

What's different in Maggy's case, one might say, is site selection. She's placing her bets for the future of the world on seventy thousand refugees living in little brick houses on the edge of a country known best for genocide.

I'm reminded of something I learned years ago, as an undergraduate in a class on Native American studies at the University of Montana. The professor informed us that the Black Hills of South Dakota are the geographical center of North America. He offered this tidbit of knowledge as more than trivia. He wanted us to marvel at the fact that the Black Hills are an especially sacred place for the Lakota and also a site of intense interest for late-arriving settlers of the American West.

For the Lakota, this small island mountain range is "the heart of everything that is."[7] For settlers, the Black Hills have been the site of a gold rush (in the 1870s), the chosen place for the chiseled faces of four presidents (at Mount Rushmore, starting in the 1920s), and significant uranium deposits (discovered in the 1950s). As the professor hoped, I did marvel that a single place could attract such attention from two entirely different cultures for such distinct reasons. Could it be that some mysterious energy had pooled in this place and created the center of balance for an entire continent?

I learned later that the geographical center of North America is in fact about 250 miles northeast of the Black Hills, out on the plains of North Dakota where the most remarkable feature is a large coal mine that has stripped away fifteen square miles of the earth's surface since 1970—perhaps a fitting center for a continent so rich in fossil fuels.[8] My professor's miscalculation, however, did not dissuade me from the mysterious persuasiveness of the idea that what we call *the world* might find its center of balance in certain places.

That's a hard thought to hold without it becoming biblical. Jerusalem comes to mind, of course, and so does Mecca. According to Islamic tradition, Hagar and Ishmael, whom Abraham sent off into the dessert, are buried there, near the center of the Great Mosque. But when I say it's hard not to think biblically about a geographical center, it's not a particular place I have in mind. I'm thinking instead of the overarching biblical narrative and its consistent focus on remnants (Noah and the Ark, Joseph in Egypt, refugees in exile) and margins (widows, orphans, the poor, starving prophets in the desert).

The thought that crept up on me in the prologue, as I tracked Maggy's love for Burundi back to its precolonial roots, came as a series of questions. What if the European obsession with finding the source of the Nile was a search for something more profound? What if men like Speke and Stanley were drawn to something more than a river or a lake? What if, without knowing it, they were searching for what the Lakota had already found on another continent: "the heart of everything that is"? And what if that was in Burundi?

It turns out, arguably at least, that the true source of the Nile is in Burundi. Baumann recognized this on his expedition into Burundi in 1892. "We followed the Ruvuvu upstream. After a few hours we reached a place where the valley forks and two small rivulets, barely half a meter wide, join. Here the natives were divided as to which of the two sources should be called Ruvuvu. But this seemed to me to be of secondary importance. We were standing at the source of the Kagera. We were standing at the source of the Nile."[9] What if they were also standing at a place where the world finds its center?

Such a place, in the logic of the biblical narrative, would be the remnant of a wonder-producing paradise. It would probably be a place filled with widows and orphans. Certainly, it would be a place afflicted with poverty. It might even be one of the poorest countries in the world. Most likely, it would be an obscure place, one most people haven't heard of and can't find on a map. Without question, it would be a place at the margins, on the edges, and thus a place of hope.

Acknowledgments

Let me start where others often end—with Nancy, my wife of thirty-five years and counting. As Lois Welch, wife of acclaimed Blackfoot author James Welch, once said, living with a writer is like living with a refrigerator: the door is closed, but you know it's going all the time. Nancy would agree and add that it's more fun to live with a refrigerator. I am deeply grateful to Nancy for persevering when I disappeared behind a door—literally and figuratively—to write this book.

Maggy will tell you again and again that what lasts is love. On one occasion, she offered me that message as personal advice: "I must give you this advice because I am your elder. In your life, you must learn to stop. You fall in love, but you don't take the time to wonder about the wonder of love." I replied, "What do you do, what have you done, to help people learn to love?" Maggy laughed. "Nobody can teach love. It's like trying to teach God. Nobody can teach that. It's life."

Nancy would assure you that I continue to need that advice, and I'm grateful to her for understanding better than I do that God and love are life—and for living in a way that is exemplary of both. I should add that when Maggy comes to visit, it's Nancy who takes her to daily Mass. Of Nancy, Maggy says, "She understands my faith." I'm grateful for that, and for the relationship she and Maggy have developed without me getting in the way.

Let me offer thanks to others in roughly chronological order. Emmanuel Katongole introduced me to Maggy and to Africa, and to the work of Sara Lawrence-Lightfoot and Jessica

Hoffmann Davis on portraiture. He also graciously agreed to write the foreword. Emmanuel Ndikumana introduced me to Burundi in 2009, on a memorable drive from Bujumbura to Ruyigi and back. Greg Jones, in his role as dean of Duke Divinity School, funded my trips back and forth to East Africa, and beyond that supported my writing with years of encouragement. Richard Nijimbere and Emery Emerimana were gracious hosts when I visited Maison Shalom.

Farr Curlin pushed me to write something definitive about Maggy so that he could use it in his classes before she came to Duke for a visit. That initial effort led to this book. Rick Lischer read an early draft and made invaluable comments. He also connected me to his agent, John Thornton, who succeeded in getting an earlier draft in front of editors at many of the big trade publishing houses, accruing a series of rejections. As odd as it sounds, I found them encouraging. Jason Byassee finally helped Maggy's story find a home by connecting me to Lil Copan at Orbis Books, and the book is better because of Lil's editorial work. Two of my colleagues in the Kenan Institute for Ethics at Duke were invaluable contributors: Christian Ferney designed the cover, and Laura Pinto-Coelho lent her careful eye to every word.

In the spirit of portraiture as I describe it in the preface, I didn't reach out often to others in Maggy's orbit the way many a biographer would, but Thierry Nutchey responded graciously to my queries about the cinema in Ruyigi by writing up a summary of what he remembered about its origins. And François Mairlot agreed to a joint interview with Maggy in which they remembered together how Maggy met François's wife, Véronique, and the relationship that developed from there. Maggy has many friends all around the world, but few as important in her life as Véronique and François.

When I have been with Maggy, she is often in the company of other Burundians, many of whom hosted me in one way or another. I often learned only their first names, if I learned their names at all: Aline, Ruth, Rose, Girard, Prospère. . . . Thanks to all of them, and special thanks to three others: Jean-Claude Niyonkuru, president of Fondation Maggy Barankitse; Silas Majambere, chair of the board of Maison Shalom; and Mia Gatoni, Maggy's goddaughter and a physician who once worked at Rema Hospital and now lives in Texas. All three offered me insight into Maggy's life and story that could come only from their experience as fellow refugees in the diaspora for whom Maggy has become a rallying force.

I know I'm missing the names of others who helped along the way, and I extend my apologies for the oversight. The one person I have yet to name, of course, is Maggy. She's the person who agreed to sit for this portrait for countless hours over fifteen years and to open her life to me in ways that continue to be a surprise. I hope I've lived up to her trust. I sent an earlier draft of the manuscript to Maggy. She responded to say that she had "some little corrections," but then her cancer treatment interrupted things. Despite all the time we spent together after that, we never got around to her corrections. Whatever my mistakes were, I hope some disappeared by chance in subsequent drafts. The mistakes that remain, and I'm sure there are some, are my own.

I said in the preface that I was going to attempt to capture the "full intricacies" of Maggy's life and work. Of course, my portrait is in fact partial, even when avoiding mistakes. That became readily apparent when Maggy came to visit just a few days after I had sent the final manuscript to the press. We spent almost two weeks together, and in that time so many new stories surfaced that Nancy asked me if I was recording, and Maggy joked that I was going to have to write a sequel.

Maggy told a story about meeting Burundi's vice president when he was traveling outside the country and asking him if he really thought she was a criminal. "No," he said, "that's politics." She recounted the time she met the provincial governor who had ordered the failed attempt on her life in 2007. Like Maggy, he now lives in exile in Kigali; and, while on his knees, he begged her for forgiveness. Her cousin's husband, the man who had beat her and tied her to the chair, also ended up a refugee in Kigali and came to Maggy seeking forgiveness. She declined, saying that first he would have to seek it from Lydia and Lysette. The implication was overbearing. Had he been Juliette's executioner? I couldn't bear to ask.

I was not recording. For the first time in fifteen years, I was simply listening as I would to a friend telling me a story over a cup of coffee, acutely aware of something Tracy Kidder says in *Strength in What Remains*, his book about Deogratias Niyizonkiza, another remarkable Burundian. Describing one moment in a conversation with Deo, Kidder says, "This was the Deo I didn't and couldn't know." Maggy's recent story-filled visit reminded me that there is a Maggy I don't and can't know. What I've offered here is the story of the Maggy I do and can know, and I'll be forever grateful to Maggy for letting me tell it.

A Note on Sources

My account of Maggy Barankitse is drawn primarily from formal interviews that I or others conducted between 2009 and 2024, as well as from the notes of many informal conversations I have had with Maggy. I have also relied on three published accounts that tell parts of Maggy's story: Emmanuel Katongole, "Gathering the Fragments of a New Future: Maggy Barankitse and Maison Shalom," in *The Sacrifice of Africa: A Political Theology for Africa* (Grand Rapids: William B. Eerdmans, 2011), 166–97; Emmanuel Katongole, "Maggy Barankitse and the Politics of Forgiveness in Burundi," in *Born from Lament: The Theology and Politics of Hope in Africa* (Grand Rapids: William B. Eerdmans, 2017), 225–42; and Christel Martin, *La haine n'aura pas le dernier mot: Maggy la femme aux 10000 enfants* (Paris: Albin Michel, 2005). In addition, two documentaries by the French filmmaker Thierry Nutchey were especially helpful—*L'armée des anges* (2000) and *Le cinéma des anges* (2004)—as was Thierry himself via a series of emails in April 2022. Occasionally, I draw from one of the many accounts of Maggy that can be found online. When I do, I note the source.

One result of the aesthetic nature of the method I describe in the preface is my departure from using only verbatim quotations. All my conversations with Maggy have taken place in English, which Maggy speaks with flights into French, with French syntax, and in a staccato way that sometimes leads her to stop speaking in the middle of a thought. Sometimes to convey what Maggy has said I have had to reconstruct her words from a combination of transcripts, my notes from our informal conversations, and my own memory. Generally, when I am quoting someone other than Maggy, I am reciting that person's words as Maggy recited them. When that is not the case, I have included the source in a note. Also as an aesthetic matter, I do not use ellipses for skipped words when I am quoting others, but in the notes I do record the various places I am drawing from in the text in question.

A few words about Tutsi and Hutu and about various terms in the prologue. In Swahili, a Bantu language heavily influenced by Arabic, *wa-*, when used in a word for people, indicates plural. For example, *mtu* is "person" and *watu* is "people." Swahili was—and is—the *lingua franca* of eastern Africa and the language Speke, Baumann, and others were drawing on when they used names for local populations: Warundi, Wahuma, Watusi, Wahutu, and so on. The *wa* indicates that they were speaking of a people in the plural.

In Kirundi and Kinyarwanda, also Bantu languages, the prefix *ba-* serves the same function. It has become standard in English, however, to drop these prefixes when speaking of Tutsi and Hutu. When I am quoting original sources like Speke and Baumann, I keep Watusi (and Watussi and Watutsi) and Wahutu, but otherwise I use Tutsi and Hutu for both the singular and the plural. When I draw on sources like Speke or Baumann, I have kept original spellings.

All translations of French and German are my own, but since my proficiency in both has lapsed considerably over the years, I have also relied on mechanical translators like Google Translate.

Notes

Preface

1. Jasmina Šopova, "Mama Maggy and Her 20,000 Children: A Meeting with Maggy Barankitse," *The UNESCO Courier*, April–June 2011, 21.

2. Sara Lawrence-Lightfoot and Jessica Hoffmann Davis, *The Art and Science of Portraiture* (San Francisco: Jossey-Bass Publishers, 1997), 3, 25, 12 (emphasis in the original).

3. Lawrence-Lightfoot and Davis, *Art and Science of Portraiture*, xv.

4. Christopher Vourlias, "A Land of Milk and Honey," *Greek to Me* (blog), January 28, 2010, https://postcardjunky.wordpress.com/2010/01/28/a-land-of-milk-and-honey/.

Prologue

1. For details on the search for the Nile, I have drawn on Candice Millard, *River of the Gods: Genius, Courage, and Betrayal in the Search for the Source of the Nile* (New York: Anchor Books, 2022); Tim Jeal, *Livingstone*, rev. ed. (New Haven, CT: Yale University Press, 2013), and Tim Jeal, *Stanley: The Impossible Life of Africa's Greatest Explorer* (New Haven, CT: Yale University Press, 2007).

2. Richard F. Burton, *The Lake Regions of Central Africa: A Picture of Exploration* (New York: Harper and Brothers, 1860), 307.

3. Burton, *Lake Regions*, 346.

4. Burton, *Lake Regions*, 347.

5. Henry M. Stanley, *How I Found Livingstone: Travels, Adventures, and Discoveries in Central Africa* (New York: Scribner, Armstrong & Company, 1872), 496.

6. Stanley, *Livingstone*, 480.

7. Stanley, *Livingstone*, 481.

8. Stanley, *Livingstone*, 502.

9. See Jean-Pierre Chrétien, *The Great Lakes of Africa: Two Thousand Years of History*, trans. Scott Straus (New York: Zone Books, 2003), 212–13, and Jean-Pierre Chrétien, "The Slave Trade in Burundi and Rwanda at the Beginning of German Colonisation, 1890–1896," in *Slavery in the Great Lakes Region of East Africa*, ed. Henri Médard and Shane Doyle (Oxford, UK: James Currey, 2007), 213.

10. John Hanning Speke, *Journal of the Discovery of the Source of the Nile* (New York: Harper & Brothers, 1864), 241.

11. For a history of the Hamitic hypothesis, see Edith R. Sanders, "The Hamitic Hypothesis: Its Origin and Functions in Time Perspective," *Journal of African History* 10, no. 4 (1969): 521–32.

12. Speke, *Source of the Nile*, 241, 244.

13. Oskar Baumann, *Durch Massailand zur Nilquelle: Reisen und Forschungen der Massai-Expedition des deutschen Antisklaverei-Komite in den Jahren 1891–1893* (Berlin: Hoefer & Vohsen, 1894), 77. It's noteworthy that Baumann's book includes an appendix (359–62) titled "Untersuchung von acht Schädeln" (Examination of eight skulls) by Prof. Dr. Zuckerkandl, a comparative study of four Watussi skulls with those of two Massai and two Iraqis—a clear example of the creation of ethnicity and the racialization of the Tutsi.

14. Baumann, *Durch Massailand zur Nilquelle*, 82, 84–85.

15. Baumann, *Durch Massailand zur Nilquelle*, 92.

16. Gustav Adolf von Götzen, *Durch Afrika von Ost nach West: Resultate und Begebenheiten einer Reise von der Deutsch-Ostafrikanischen Küste bis zur Kongomündung in den Jahren 1893/94* (Berlin: Dietrich Reimer, 1895), 156, 164, 171, 189.

17. Götzen, *Durch Afrika von Ost nach West*, 188, 156, 190–91, 160.

18. Lothar von Trotha, *Meine Bereisung von Deutsch-Ostafrika* (Berlin: B. Brigl, 1897), 72. See also Roger Botte, "Rwanda and Burundi, 1889–1930: Chronology of a Slow Assassination, Part 1," *International Journal of African Historical Studies* 18, no. 1 (1985): 53–91; and Hans von Ramsay, "Uha, Urundi, und Ruanda: Nach einem vorläufigen Bericht des Hauptmanns Ramsay," in *Mittheilungen von Forschungs-*

reisenden und Gelehrten aus den deutschen Schutzgebieten, vol. 10, ed. Freiherr von Danckelman (Berlin: Ernst Siegfried Mittler und Sohn, 1897), 77–78.

19. Ramsay, "Uha, Urundi, und Ruanda," 78.

20. Heinrich von Bethe, as quoted in Botte, "Rwanda and Burundi," 77–78.

21. Botte, "Rwanda and Burundi," 78.

22. Botte, "Rwanda and Burundi," 79.

23. Chrétien, *The Great Lakes of Africa*, 201.

Part 1: (East of) Eden

1. The final verses do not appear on the memorial but are in keeping with Maggy's worldview: "for it is in giving that one receives, / it is in self-forgetting that one finds, / it is in pardoning that one is pardoned, / it is in dying that one is raised to eternal life." The prayer was mistakenly attributed to St. Francis but in fact appeared the first time in 1912 in a French magazine and became especially popular, sometimes set to music, during World War I and World War II: "Wikipedia: Prayer of St. Francis," Wikimedia Foundation, last modified September 9, 2024, https://en.wikipedia.org/wiki/Prayer_of_Saint_Francis.

2. For background on the events of 1993, see "International Commission of Inquiry for Burundi: Final Report, 1995–1996," United States Institute of Peace, https://www.usip.org/sites/default/files/file/resources/collections/commissions/Burundi-Report.pdf.

3. The war ended formally in 2005 and is often referred to as a twelve-year war, but rebel-instigated violence continued through 2008. A count of 300,000 dead is common in the press; no accurate number exists. Data from this period tracked by the Institute for Health Metrics and Evaluation suggest more than 236,000 deaths from HIV/AIDS alone (https://vizhub.healthdata.org/gbd-compare/). On the number of orphans at the end of the war in 2005, see *Africa's Orphaned and Vulnerable Generations: Children Affected by AIDS* (New York: United Nations Children's Fund, 2006), 36.

4. René Lemarchand, *The Dynamics of Violence in Central Africa* (Philadelphia: University of Pennsylvania Press, 2009), 129.

5. Michael Bowen et al., *Passing By: The United States and Genocide in Burundi, 1972* (Carnegie Endowment for International Peace, 1973), 1.

6. René Lemarchand, "The Burundian Killings of 1972," SciencesPo, June 27, 2008, https://www.sciencespo.fr/mass-violence-war-massacre-resistance/en/document/burundi-killings-1972.html.

7. Aidan Russell, *Politics and Violence in Burundi: The Language of Truth in an Emerging State* (Cambridge, UK: Cambridge University Press, 2019), 49.

8. Jean-Pierre Chrétien, *The Great Lakes of Africa: Two Thousand Years of History*, trans. Scott Straus (New York: Zone Books, 2003), 304.

9. Lemarchand, *Dynamics of Violence*, 47.

10. Russell, *Politics and Violence in Burundi*, 44.

11. On the Bashingantahe, see Pacifique Irankunda, *The Tears of a Man Flow Inward* (New York: Random House, 2022), esp. 26–31.

12. Maggy's mother was perhaps adapting a Burundian proverb: "A man who tells no lies cannot feed his child"; recorded in Christel Martin, *La haine n'aura pas le dernier mot: Maggy la femme aux 10000 enfants* (Paris: Albin Michel, 2005), 17.

13. Tara Zahra, *The Lost Children: Reconstructing Europe's Families after World War II* (Cambridge, MA: Harvard University Press, 2011), 3–4.

14. Quoted in Joseph Wechsberg, "Profile: A House Called Peace," *New Yorker*, December 22, 1962, 39.

15. Gmeiner once said, "I have no illusion. Even if we grow and grow we can accept only a very small number of the children who need our help." When he died in 1986, there were 230 children's villages around the world. By 2013 there were 554, populated by 82,000 children. Things have plateaued since, with 559 villages in 2022. See SOS Children's Villages, https://www.sos-childrensvillages.org.

16. On the religious demographics of Burundi at this time, see Léonce Segamba et al., *Enquête démographique et de santé au Burundi, 1987* (Gitega, Burundi: Ministère de l'Intérieur Département de la Population, 1988), 11.

17. On Bagaza and the Catholic Church, see Lemarchand, *Burundi: Ethnic Conflict and Genocide* (Cambridge, UK: Woodrow Wilson Center Press, 1996), 112–14.

18. It's perhaps not incidental that the United Nations published *Our Common Future*, now known famously as the Brundtland Report, just as Maggy was arriving in Switzerland in 1987: *Our Common Future: Report of the World Commission on Environment and Development* (Geneva: United Nations, 1987). This report put "sustainable development" on the global agenda for the first time. Maggy has never made the connection explicit, but this context helps explain her shift in trajectory from schoolteacher to practitioner of economic development, a shift that involved two more years of education.

19. For a good account of events in 1993 and into the mid-1990s, see Robert and Kathleen Krueger, *From Bloodshed to Hope in Burundi: Our Embassy Years during Genocide* (Austin: University of Texas Press, 2007). Robert Krueger was the U.S. ambassador to Burundi from May 1994 to September 1995 and served heroically in that capacity by traveling the country documenting genocide, until he was called back by Washington following a failed assassination attempt.

20. Chloé Ndayikunda, speaking in the documentary *L'armée des anges* (2000), directed by Thierry Nutchey and Joseph Bitamba. There are conflicting details about what transpired when Maggy was reunited with her own children. In *L'armée des anges*, Chloé goes on to say, "I had to step over dead bodies, there were wounded people screaming. I found children among them and finally we found Maggy who had also recovered other children." This account makes it appear that she left her hiding place in the sacristy and found Maggy outside, a significant departure from Maggy's version. In *La haine n'aura pas le dernier mot*, Martin describes yet a different scene, in which Chloé and the other children, having escaped in some undisclosed fashion, arrive in the back of a truck and find a distraught Maggy in the compound. The version I tell here is the one I have heard repeatedly and consistently from Maggy herself.

21. Reports of the number of dead vary. Maggy herself uses a much larger number. I am using the number as reported in "Human Rights Watch World Report – 1997," UNHCR, https://www.refworld.org/docid/3ae6a8ad2o.html.

22. Quoting and paraphrasing, "320 Tutsis Killed in Attack on Displaced Persons Camp," July 23, 1996, OCHA, ReliefWeb, https://

reliefweb.int/report/burundi/320-tutsis-killed-attack-displaced-persons-camp.

23. Hugh Dellios, "Ethnic Genocide Grips Burundi," *Chicago Tribune*, July 22, 1996. Four months earlier, Jonathan Frerichs had used a similar phrase; see "Saving Burundi," *Christian Century*, March 6, 1996, 252–54. The other notable event during this time occurred on July 25, two days after the mass burial in Bugendana, when the Tutsi general Pierre Buyoya took over the country in a coup, something he had done before, in 1987, after which he then ruled the country as the chairman of a military junta for six years. It's likely that Buyoya was behind Ndadaye's assassination in October 1993, and thus the cause of the violence that was now entrenched as an ethnic civil war. His return to power did not bode well for what was to come. See Krueger and Krueger, *From Bloodshed to Hope*, esp. 266–71.

24. For a summary of these months in 1996, see "Human Rights Watch World Report—1997"; Bob Drogin, "New U.N. Report Reveals Hidden Burundi Killings," *Washington Post*, August 4, 1996.

25. Maggy herself has offered different years for the creation of La Cité des Anges, ranging from 1997 to 2000—sometimes, it seems, not making a distinction between when something arrived in her imagination and when she brought it to life, and sometimes connecting this event to the wrong moment in the drawn-out peace process that she sometimes uses as a chronological reference. The year in question was also difficult to pin down because Martin says it was 2002 (*La haine n'aura pas le dernier mot*, 176), as does the website for the documentary *Le cinéma des anges*, Thierry Nutchey: Le cinéma des anges, http://africanistes.org/evenement/thierry-nutchey-cinema-anges. The documentary itself, however, clearly states the year as 2003. I was able to confirm the date of April 2003 via a series of email exchanges with Thierry Nutchey, April 5–11, 2022. Other sources that describe what was happening in Ruyigi on April 16 and 17 in 2003 were also helpful; see "OCHA-Burundi Situation Report 14–20 Apr 2003," April 20, 2003, ReliefWeb, https://reliefweb.int/report/burundi/ocha-burundi-situation-report-14-20-apr-2003; and Henri Boshoff, "Burundi: The African Union's First Mission, African Security Analysis Programme Situation Report," June 10, 2003, Insti-

tute for Security Studies, https://issafrica.s3.amazonaws.com/site/uploads/BURUNDIJUN03.PDF.

26. "Arusha Peace and Reconciliation Agreement for Burundi," August 28, 2000, Peace Accords Matrix, https://peaceaccords.nd.edu/accord/arusha-peace-and-reconciliation-agreement-for-burundi. The eventual president was Pierre Nkurunziza, the top commander of the CNDD-FDD (*Conseil national pour la défense de la démocratie—Forces pour la défense de la démocratie*), which by August 2000 had split into three factions, with Nkurunziza battling to control the largest. For helpful context, see Paul Nantulya, "Burundi: Why the Arusha Accords Are Central," August 5, 2015, Africa Center for Strategic Studies, https://africacenter.org/spotlight/burundi-why-the-arusha-accords-are-central/: "The mediation team barred [Nkurunziza] from the negotiating table until he reconciled his movement and negotiated with one voice, a demand that his fellow commanders considered 'patronizing.' The movement's relationship with the mediation team as well as with regional countries became increasingly acrimonious. As a result, the movement remained outside the Arusha negotiations and did not sign the Accords."

27. Quoting and paraphrasing, "U.S. Department of State Country Report on Human Rights Practices 2003—Burundi," February 25, 2004, UNHCR, https://www.refworld.org/docid/403f57aec.html.

28. Speaking in the documentary *Le cinéma des anges*.

29. Speaking in the documentary *Le cinéma des anges*. For April attacks on provincial capitals, see "Transition in Burundi: Time to Deliver," April 30, 2003, Human Rights Watch, https://www.hrw.org/legacy/backgrounder/africa/burundi/burundi043003-bck.pdf. For reference to the April 17 attack on Ruyigi, see "OCHA-Burundi Situation Report 14–20 Apr 2003."

30. See Wechsberg, "A House Called Peace," 42, 47–48.

31. Quoted in Martin, *La haine n'aura pas le dernier mot*, 155.

32. Speaking in the documentary *Le cinéma des anges*.

33. Speaking in the documentary *Le cinéma des anges*.

34. Email exchanges with Thierry Nutchey, April 5–11, 2022. Thierry was working for the French production company Loreleï. The six-film series was titled *Visage du Burundi*, directed by the Burundian director Joseph Bitamba (who later co-directed *L'armée*

des anges) and co-produced by Radio Télévision Nationale du Burundi (RTNB). "We shot with the means of the RTNB and a very small local team in very difficult conditions, with this war and a camera which always broke down."

35. Chloé Ndayikunda, speaking in the documentary *L'armée des anges*.

36. Martin, *La haine n'aura pas le dernier mot*, 166.

37. Quoted in Martin, *La haine n'aura pas le dernier mot*, 131. Martin's account of Maggy's discovery of Dieudonné on the streets of Butezi differs from the one I have heard directly from Maggy.

38. Robert Pogue Harrison, *The Dominion of the Dead* (Chicago: University of Chicago Press, 2003), 122–23.

39. Harrison, *Dominion of the Dead*, xi.

40. See Annalee Newitz, *Four Lost Cities: A Secret History of the Urban Age* (New York: W. W. Norton, 2021), 19–75. For a wider look at Neolithic burial practices, see Goce Naumov, "Housing the Dead: Burials inside Houses and Vessels in the Neolithic Balkans," in *Cult in Context: Reconsidering Ritual in Archaeology*, ed. David Barrowclough and Caroline Malone (Oxford: Oxbow Books, 2007), 255–56. For a broad overview of the role the dead have played and continue to play in the formation of culture, especially in the Christian West, see Thomas W. Laqueur, *The Work of the Dead: A Cultural History of Mortal Remains* (Princeton, NJ: Princeton University Press, 2015). On the relics of saints, see Peter Brown, *The Cult of the Saints: Its Rise and Function in Latin Christianity* (Chicago: University of Chicago Press, 1981). For an interesting account of altars and hearths in ancient Rome that makes their connections to ancestors more complicated than has often been assumed in the past, see Harriet I. Flower, *The Dancing Lares and the Serpent in the Garden: Religion at the Roman Street Corner* (Princeton, NJ: Princeton University Press, 2017).

41. Harrison, *Dominion of the Dead*, 22.

42. Harrison, *Dominion of the Dead*, 158–59.

43. Translating the French that appears on the memorial: ICI REPOSENT LES 72 VICTIMES DU 24 10 1993. CHERS PARENTS, CHERS AMIS, REPOSEZ VOUS EN PAIX!

44. Michael Barnett, *Empire of Humanity: A History of Humanitarianism* (Ithaca, NY: Cornell University Press, 2011), 27.

Part 2: Exile

1. "Arusha Peace and Reconciliation Agreement for Burundi," August 28, 2000, Peace Accords Matrix, https://peaceaccords.nd.edu/accord/arusha-peace-and-reconciliation-agreement-for-burundi.

2. "Burundi: Violence, Rights Violations Mar Elections," July 1, 2010, Human Rights Watch, https://www.hrw.org/news/2010/07/01/burundi-violence-rights-violations-mar-elections.

3. "Parliament Rejects the Constitutional Revision," March 25, 2014, Agenzia Fides, https://www.fides.org/en/news/35460-AFRICA_BURUNDI_Parliament_rejects_the_Constitutional_Revision.

4. Stephanie M. Burchard, "Burundi 2015: Nkurunziza Prepares Ground for a Third Term," April 10, 2014, African Arguments, https://africanarguments.org/2014/04/burundi-2015-nkurunziza-prepares-ground-for-a-third-term-by-dr-stephanie-m-burchard/.

5. Stef Vandeginste, "Legal Loopholes and the Politics of Executive Term Limits: Insights from Burundi," *Africa Spectrum* 51, no. 2 (2016): 39–63; Tomas Van Acker, "Understanding Burundi's Predicament," *Africa Policy Brief* 11 (June 2015): 1–10.

6. Lt. Gen. Roméo Dallaire, with Maj. Brent Beardsley, *Shake Hands with the Devil: The Failure of Humanity in Rwanda* (Cambridge, MA: De Capo Press, 2003), xxv.

7. "Case History: Pierre Claver Mbonimpa," Frontline Defenders, https://www.frontlinedefenders.org/en/case/case-history-pierre-claver-mbonimpa.

8. "Burundi: May 2014 Monthly Forecast," May 1, 2014, Security Council Report, https://www.securitycouncilreport.org/monthly-forecast/2014-05/burundi_4.php; and on the Imbonerakure, see "Who Are the Imbonerakure and Is Burundi Unravelling?," April 28, 2015, The New Humanitarian, https://www.thenewhumanitarian.org/news/2015/04/28/who-are-imbonerakure-and-burundi-unravelling.

9. Vandeginste, "Legal Loopholes."

10. "Fighting for Human Rights in Burundi: An Interview with Bob Rugurika," January 21, 2016, Freedom House, https://freedomhouse.org/article/fighting-human-rights-burundi-interview-bob-rugurika.

11. "Jean-Népomuscène Komezamahoro: A Cheerful Young Life

Stolen by a Police Bullet in Burundi," October 5, 2018, Amnesty International, https://www.amnesty.org/en/latest/campaigns/2018/10/jean-nepomuscene-komezamahoro-a-cheerful-young-life-stolen-by-a-police-bullet-in-burundi/.

12. Elaine Sciolino, "Maria Teresa and Marguerite Barankitse, Worlds Apart, Help Victims of Rape," *New York Times*, March 8, 2019.

13. UN Human Rights Council, "Detailed Final Report of the Commission of Inquiry on Burundi," September 29, 2017, unofficial translation from French, https://www.ohchr.org/en/hr-bodies/hrc/co-i-burundi/co-i-burundi-report-hrc36.

14. UNICEF, "Burundi: Humanitarian Situation Report," July 31, 2016; and "Rwanda Fact Sheet," July 2016, https://www. unhcr. org/rw/sites/rw/files/legacy-pdf/UNHCR-Rwanda-Monthly-Fact sheet-July-2016.pdf.

15. For details about Richard Nijimbere and Maison Shalom here and below, I am drawing on Richard Nijimbere, interview with the author, July 21, 2016, Kigali, Rwanda.

16. "Press Release on the Suspension of Ten (10) Non-governmental Organizations in Burundi," December 3, 2015, ReliefWeb, https://reliefweb.int/report/burundi/press-release-suspension-ten-10-non-governmental-organizations-burundi.

17. UN Human Rights Council, "Detailed Final Report."

18. Anthony Slide, ed., *Ravished Armenia and the Story of Aurora Mardiganian* (Jackson: University Press of Mississippi, 2014), 1.

19. Quoted in Samantha Power, *"A Problem from Hell": America and the Age of Genocide* (New York: Basic Books, 2013), 17.

20. "About the Aurora Prize for Awakening Humanity," Aurora Humanitarian Initiative, https://legacy.auroraprize.com/en/prize/detail/about.

21. In a novel setup, the recipient of the Aurora Prize receives $100,000 personally, and then is given access to $1 million to give away to up to three organizations of their choice.

22. "About the Opus Prize," Opus Prize, http://www.opusprize.org/about.

23. "Aurora Prize Inaugural Ceremony" (video), Aurora Humanitarian Initiative, https://auroraprize.com/en/aurora-prize-inaugural-ceremony-video-0.

24. "Burundi Bwacu," Wikimedia Foundation, last modified April 21, 2024, https://en.wikipedia.org/wiki/Burundi_Bwacu.

25. "Address of His Holiness Pope Francis," Malmö, Sweden, October 31, 2016, The Holy See, https://www.vatican.va/content/francesco/en/speeches/2016/october/documents/papa-francesco_20161031_svezia-evento-ecumenico.html.

26. "Resident / Humanitarian Coordinator Report on the Use of CERF Funds, Rwanda Rapid Response Conflict-Related Displacement 2015," United Nations CERF, https://cerf.un.org/sites/default/files/resources/15-RR-RWA-15006-NR01_Rwanda_RCHC.Report_final.pdf; and International Federation of the Red Cross and Red Crescent, "Emergency Plan of Action—Final Report Rwanda: Population Movement," May 31, 2017.

27. Martina Pomeroy, "Mahama Refugee Camp, One Year On," April 22, 2016, UNHCR, https://www.unhcr.org/rw/news/press-releases/watch-video-mahama-refugee-camp-one-year#:~:text=Saber%20Azam%2C%20othe%20UNHCR%20Representative,Rwandan%20children%2C"%20Azam%20says.

28. "Burundian refugees daily updates—15 May 2015," ReliefWeb, https://reliefweb.int/report/rwanda/burundian-refugees-daily-updates-15-may-2015.

29. "Mrs. Marguerite Barankitse (Founder, Maison Shalom International) at the Subcommittee on International Human Rights," June 6, 2019, Open Parliament, https://openparliament.ca/commit tees/international-human-rights/42-1/157/marguerite-barankitse-1/only/.

Part 3: Return

1. Mireri Junior, "Burundi First Lady Hospitalised at Aga Khan after Contracting Covid-19," May 29, 2020, *The Standard*, https://www.standardmedia.co.ke/health/article/2001373190/burundi-first-lady-hospitalised-at-aga-khan-after-contracting-covid-19#google_vignette.

2. "Burundi: Events of 2021," Human Rights Watch, https://www.hrw.org/world-report/2022/country-chapters/burundi.

3. "Burundi: Condamnation in absentia à une peine de prison à perpétuité de douze défenseurs des droits humains," *Fédération*

Internationale pour les Droits Humains, February 2, 2021, https://www.fidh.org/fr/themes/defenseurs-des-droits-humains/burundi-condamnation-in-absentia-a-une-peine-de-prison-a-perpetuite.

4. UNHCR, "Rwanda: 2020 Mid-Year Report, Burundi Regional RRP," September 29, 2020, Operational Data Portal, https://data.unhcr.org/en/documents/details/79266.

5. Emery Manirambona et al., "Impact of the COVID-19 Pandemic on the Food Rations of Refugees in Rwanda," *International Journey for Equity in Health* 20 (2021), https://equityhealthj.biomedcentral.com/counter/pdf/10.1186/s12939-021-01450-1.pdf.

6. "Mission and Values," Maison Shalom International, https://maisonshalom.org/a-propos-de-nous/.

7. Maison Shalom International, *Annual Report 2021,* https://maisonshalom.org/wp-content/uploads/2022/10/ANNUAL-REPORT-2021-CORRECT-2-1.pdf.

8. François Mairlot, interview with the author, July 14, 2024, Kigali, Rwanda.

9. "OurMissions,"FondationMaggyBarankitse,https://fondationmaggy.org/nos-missions.

10. "Our Mission," International Baccalaureate, https://www.ibo.org/about-the-ib/mission/.

11. Marie-Thérèse Maurette, "Techniques d'éducation pour la paix: Existent-elles? Réponse à une enquête d'Unesco," June 5, 1948, Ecolint Alumni Network, http://alumni.ecolint.net/authors/maurette/.

12. "Constitution of the United Nations Educational, Scientific and Cultural Organization," UNESCO, last updated July 24, 2024, https://www.unesco.org/en/legal-affairs/constitution.

13. For the early history of UNESCO and its efforts in education, see early issues of its publication, *The UNESCO Courier,* esp. vol. 1, no. 1 (February 1948); vol. 2, no. 1 (February 1949); and vol. 3, no. 4 (May 1950).

14. Nelson Mandela, preface to *Mandela's Way: Lessons for an Uncertain Age,* by Richard Stengel (New York: Broadway Books, 2010), xi.

15. Desmond Tutu, "We Must Turn the Spotlight on Ourselves," in *God Is Not a Christian: And Other Provocations,* ed. John Allen (New York: HarperOne, 2011), 172.

16. Desmond Tutu, "What about Justice?" in *God Is Not a Christian*, 44.

17. *Marguerite's Fearless Journey* (2024), directed by Øystein Rakkenes.

18. Desmond Tutu, "*Ubuntu*," in *God Is Not a Christian*, 21–22.

19. *Oxford English Dictionary*, 2nd ed., s.v. "ubuntu."

20. Tutu, "*Ubuntu*," 22–23.

21. "Valeurs," L'École Sainte-Anne de Kigali, https://ecolesainte anne.org/a-propos-2/.

22. "Académie Ubuntu: Introduction," Maison Shalom International, https://maisonshalom.org/ubuntu/.

23. The website for the memorial states, "The levels of violence were significantly high in Nyarubuye, even in the context of the overall genocide"; see "Nyarubuye Memorial," Genocide Archive of Rwanda, https://genocidearchiverwanda.org.rw/index.php/Nyarubuye_Memorial. See also Nicole M. Ephgrave, "Sexual Violence at Nyarubuye: History, Justice, Memory—A Case Study of the 1994 Rwandan Genocide" (PhD diss., University of Western Ontario, 2015).

24. The story of Nyarubuye is well known thanks to its appearance as the opening story in Philip Gourevitch's *We Wish to Inform You That Tomorrow We Will Be Killed with Our Families: Stories from Rwanda* (New York: Farrar, Straus and Giroux, 1999), as well as in other popular accounts of the genocide. Despite that fact, I was not aware of its proximity to Mahama at the time of my visits to the camp, nor of the fact that the levels of violence, both in terms of intensity and numbers of death, were especially high in the region around Mahama. See David Yanagizawa-Drott's fascinating study on the role of radio broadcasts in fomenting the genocide: "Propaganda and Conflict: Evidence from the Rwandan Genocide" (2014), Zurich Open Repository and Archive, https://www.zora.uzh.ch/id/eprint/137646/1/Propaganda_and_conflict_Drott.pdf.

25. Mohsin Hamid, *Exit West* (New York: Riverhead Books, 2017). In what follows, listed in order of appearance, I am quoting, usually without ellipses, from pages 3, 68, 7–8, 30, 72–73, 88, 129, 135, 158–59, 163, 166, 169, 213, 173, 170, 217.

Epilogue

1. Thomas Keneally, *Schindler's List* (New York: Simon and Schuster, Touchstone edition, 1993), 14.

2. T. W. Adorno, *Negative Dialectics*, trans. E. B. Ashton (New York: Continuum, 1973), 364.

3. C. Kavin Rowe, "What If It Were True: Why Study the New Testament?," *New Testament Studies* 68 (2022): 144–55.

4. Here and just below, Shelly Rambo, *Spirit and Trauma: A Theology of Remaining* (Louisville, KY: Westminster John Knox Press, 2010), 157, 7.

5. Nick Romeo, "How Mondragon Became the World's Largest Co-Op," *New Yorker,* August 27, 2022.

6. See, for example, "Africa's New Cities Summit," November 16–18, 2023, Charter Cities Institute, https://chartercitiesinstitute.org/africas-new-cities-summit/; and "Africa's Rising Cities: How Africa Will Become the Center of the World's Urban Future," *Washington Post*, November 19, 2021.

7. William Greider, "The Heart of Everything That Is," *Rolling Stone*, May 7, 1987.

8. Steph Yin, "North America's Geographical Center May Be in a North Dakota Town Called Center," *New York Times*, January 25, 2017.

9. Oskar Baumann, *Durch Massailand zur Nilquelle: Reisen und Forschungen der Massai-Expedition des deutschen Antisklaverei-Komite in den Jahren 1891–1893* (Berlin: Hoefer & Vohsen, 1894), 88.